Chain Reactions

Broadly speaking, we are in the middle of a race between human skill as to means and human folly as to ends.

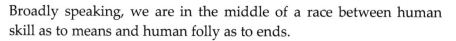

Bertrand Russell (1872-1970) 'The Impact of Science on Society'

Chain Reactions:
How the Chemical Industry Can Shrink Our Carbon Footprint

David Merlin-Jones

Foreword by

Brendan Barber

Civitas: Institute for the Study of Civil Society
London

First Published June 2011

© Civitas 2011
55 Tufton Street
London SW1P 3QL

email: books@civitas.org.uk

ISBN 978-1-906837-20-4

Typeset by
Civitas

Printed in Great Britain by

Berforts Group Ltd
Stevenage SG1 2BH

Contents

Author

David Merlin-Jones is a graduate from Exeter College, University of Oxford where he studied history. He joined Civitas in 2010 as a Research Fellow, focusing on economic issues and, in particular, British manufacturing and energy. He has authored previous Civitas reports including *Rock Solid? An investigation into the British cement industry* (2010), *The Industrial and Commercial Finance Corporation: Lessons from the past for the future* (2010) and co-authored *Economic Growth: could the Government do more?* (2011). He has also contributed to the 2009 edition of the *Civitas Review*.

Acknowledgements

The author is grateful to the following for sparing their time to be interviewed:

Fiona Ferguson, Media and Government Relations Manager at the Chemicals Industries Association; Deborah Pritchard Jones, Business Projects & Public Affairs manager at GrowHow; Jeremy Nicholson, Director of the Energy-Intensive Users Group; Dr Stan Higgins, Chief Executive of NEPIC; Phil Bailey, Cassel site director at Lucite International

In addition, the author would also like to thank the following for contributing their assistance and expertise to this publication:

Mark Lewis, Technical Manager, Northeast of England Process Industry Cluster; Lisa Waters, Director of Waters Wye; Aoife O'Donnell, Civitas; Frances Cairncross CBE, Rector of Exeter College, Oxford; and Ruth Lea, Economic Advisor and Director of Arbuthnot Banking Group plc.

List of Acronyms

BIS	Department for Business, Innovation & Skills
BRIC	Brazil, Russia, India and China
CCA	Climate Change Act
CCL	Climate Change Levy
CCS	Carbon Capture and Storage
CIA	Chemical Industries Association
CRC	Carbon Reduction Commitment Energy Efficiency Scheme
CPF	Carbon price floor
CRC	Carbon Reduction Commitment
DECC	Department for Energy and Climate Change
EU ETS	European Union Emissions Trading System
IED	Industrial Emissions Directive
GHG	Greenhouse gas
LCE	Low-carbon economy
MMA	Methyl methacrylate
NEPIC	North East of England Process Industry Cluster
OFGEM	Office of Gas and Electricity Markets
REACH	Registration, Evaluation and Authorisation and Restriction of Chemicals
RHI	Renewable Heat Incentive
RO	Renewables Obligation
SME	Small & medium sized enterprises
STEM	Science, technology, engineering and mathematics
WID	Waste Incineration Directive
WRAP	Waste & Resources Action Programme

Foreword

Energy-intensive industries—chemicals, iron and steel, aluminium, cement and lime manufacture, pulp and paper making - together employ some 225,000 people in the UK, many in highly skilled occupations. Offering good quality, union negotiated terms and conditions, these industries account directly for about one per cent of UK GDP (some £15 billion), and much more in supply chains. In view of concerns over the industrial costs of energy policies linked to climate change, the focus of *Chain Reactions*, the TUC was pleased to sponsor an independent study jointly with the Energy Intensive Users Group (EIUG) in 2010. Both sponsors firmly support the shift to a low-carbon economy as an essential response to the challenge of climate change. We also believe that the energy-intensive industries are vital to the success of this transition.

As *Chain Reactions* shows, the chemical industry has reduced its CO_2 emissions by 75 per cent in eighteen years, from about $48MtCO_2e$ in 1990 to around $13MtCO_2e$ in 2008. It can hardly be said to have dragged its heels. To enable energy-intensive industries to participate in the creation of an efficient low-carbon economy, they require policies that underpin equitable burden-sharing for the associated costs between all sectors; domestic, commercial and industrial. So the purpose of the TUC/EIUG report was to open an evidence-based and informed discussion on the effects of climate change policies on the UK's energy-intensive sectors.

Based on the data provided by a representative cross-section of companies, the study's consultants, Waters Wye Associates, estimated the increase in overall energy bills, including all of the climate change policies that attach to energy bills, along with the EU Emissions Trading System (EU ETS) Phase III exposure that companies would directly face. The results showed that:

- The impact of the various electricity-based charges will increase total electricity bills by between 15 per cent and 22 per cent by 2020. This does not include the costs of EU ETS phase III.

- The increase in total gas bills resulting from these schemes will be between 20 per cent and 22 per cent by 2020. Again, this does not include the costs of EU ETS phase III.

- The forecast increase in the total energy bill, taking electricity, gas and emissions reductions schemes together is projected to be between 18 per cent and 141 per cent. These figures include the costs of EU ETS phase III.

The cumulative impact of all climate change policies is significant, especially on energy-intensive sectors. It concluded that: 'If the government continues to simply add one energy or carbon reduction levy after another on to the energy-intensive sectors then the risk is that these industries will no longer be able to compete internationally and will simply cease to operate in the UK.'

The current review of the UK's energy market appears to have missed the significance of the TUC/EIUG study. The energy review is taking place against the backdrop of a faltering economy, rising unemployment and fuel poverty. The Energy Market Reform (EMR) should therefore be seen as a prime opportunity to deliver green jobs growth and affordable energy. Yet this energy review seems disconnected from the urgent need to create jobs and provide energy at prices that industry and domestic consumers can afford.

The electricity market should operate first and foremost in the national interest. The TUC recognises the need to introduce an effective price of carbon emissions, to drive investment and jobs in low-carbon technology. But such a policy has consequences that are not addressed in the EMR. As the TUC has pointed out, the review looks set to increase energy costs and threaten investment and jobs in our energy-intensive industries, while hard pressed domestic consumers face rising energy bills. It is likely to increase our dependence on imported gas at the expense of our massive domestic coal reserves, while there are real dangers that the UK will lose this opportunity for world leadership in carbon capture technology, and the opportunity to create skilled jobs in carbon capture-related technology (itself essentially a chemical process) by 2020.

Surprisingly, given the evidence published jointly by the TUC and the Energy-intensive Users Group in 2010, the costs impact of this latest energy policy review on the energy-intensive sectors has not so far been factored into government thinking.

It is vital at this crucial moment in energy policy making, that government strikes the right balance between its climate change and industrial polices. If we get this wrong, then the industrial damage may be irreparable. If these sectors do not remain in the UK, future UK demand for energy-intensive products will be met by imports from countries with less demanding fiscal environments at the expense of UK jobs and controls on CO_2 emissions: carbon leakage will result. Economic growth and tax revenues will suffer. But if we get this balance right, then the UK stands to be world leader in low-carbon goods and services that the chemicals sectors is well placed to deliver.

Brendan Barber, General Secretary of the TUC

Preface

The issues affecting the chemicals sector as investigated in this publication are inextricably tied up with the issue of climate change. How far this is a problem and the extent to which it is anthropogenic are still hotly debated topics. This study will not delve into the debate but it assumes that climate change is a real threat to the future of humanity and that it is in part a man-made phenomenon. On that basis, it is assumed that there is something humans can do to mitigate climate change by minimising the pollution that human activity causes.

Even those who do not subscribe to the view that global warming is man-made are unlikely to argue that squandering the Earth's finite resources is a positive thing or that the fledgling industries supplying low-carbon innovations are not beneficial to the wider economy. As such, they too would have to agree that it is desirable for British industries such as the chemicals sector to increase their efficiency and thereby reduce their emissions. The real issue is *how* this is done.

This paper focuses on the British chemicals sector because current climate change and energy related policies look set to inflict serious damage on it in the near future. The key issue is that the government's present policies are not the only way to reduce climate change: there are other, far less damaging ways to achieve this. Shrinking the UK's carbon footprint does not have to be a sackcloth-and-ashes affair in which vast swathes of the economy are sacrificed. Helping these existing sectors evolve to fit the low-carbon economy is the real route out of the crisis.

It should also be remembered that global warming affects all nations and all humanity. Britain accounts for two per cent of emissions, so reducing these alone, however laudable, is ultimately futile. Taking an international perspective clearly shows that supporting rather than undermining the British chemicals sector would be far more useful in the fight against climate change.

Summary

The Coalition Government's *Growth Review* and the 2011 Budget set out an agenda that aims to foster both economic growth and a low-carbon economy. Despite the tough economic environment, the self-proclaimed 'greenest government ever' is continuing and advancing the previous government's green levies and taxes, suggesting that economic growth is secondary to low-carbon goals and under-mining both aims in the process.

The Climate Change Act has committed Britain to reducing emissions by 34 per cent from 1990 levels by 2020, the deepest cut of any industrialised nation. These reductions are being made through high charges on emissions and energy use. Those most affected by this are energy-intensive industries whose Achilles' heel are power overheads—one chemical firm uses more energy than Liverpool and Manchester combined. The outcome of rising energy costs will be the bankruptcy of small and medium sized enterprises (SMEs), the emigration of larger firms and a long-term decline in foreign investment in the UK. Yet the chemical sector is the foundation of the low-carbon economy.

The importance of the chemical sector

This study investigates how climate-change related policies will affect the chemical industry. This sector was chosen on the basis of its unique benefits. In economic terms:

- It is a £60 billion industry and contributed £17.1bn gross value added to the economy in 2009 using 2006 prices.

- It is responsible for 15 per cent of British exports and is the only sector with a positive trade balance.

- It directly employs 200,000 highly skilled workers with a further 400,000 dependent on a UK chemical industry.

Furthermore, the chemical industry is environmentally important and part of the solution to climate change, rather than the problem:

- While the chemicals sector may be carbon-intensive, it forms the basis of the low-carbon economy, producing the raw materials needed for a range of green products, from energy-efficient catalysts to insulators.

- The sector's average emissions saving ratio is 2:1—two tonnes of CO_2 saved down the line for every tonne emitted in production

- The highly specialised skills needed by the chemicals sector are near identical to those required by low-carbon industries.

The troubled mentality of the Coalition Government's policies

The philosophy behind the government's approach to cutting climate change through pressuring the chemical sector is essentially flawed: it assumes the industry does not care how much it emits. This approach is negative, all stick and no carrot. However, the sector is no longer the dirty and dangerous heavy industry it was in the past and, while energy-intensive, it is energy-efficient. The industry has every incentive to minimise its largest overhead to stay competitive, even without climate-change policies.

Key problems with current policy

The government is failing to provide the positive impetus for industry that other countries are delivering. It assumes that encouraging the chemical industry and manufacturing and cutting emissions are mutually exclusive choices. This is not the case. Without the chemicals sector and its products, important emission-reducing technology would vanish from the UK. Significant issues are:

- The fight against greenhouse gas (GHG) emissions is not a sprint but a marathon. The previous government signed up to unrealistic targets and the present one is aiming to cut the UK's carbon emissions as much as possible in the lifetime of this parliament. The pre-occupation with targets for 2020 relies on energy-intensive sectors disappearing from the UK's emission balance sheet. This approach is misguided as it relies on forcing out the industries that will help reach the 80 per cent reduction by 2050 and beyond. The government should not focus on winning short-term environmental brownie points at the expense of long-term low-carbon development.

- In the medium-term, Britain will have a mixed-carbon economy, reliant on renewable and fossil fuel sources. The technology for an entirely low-carbon economy does not yet exist and will take time to develop, no matter how punishing energy charges become. This reality must be acknowledged.

- The government expects the low-carbon economy to develop from 'new' industries that need to be funded and incentivised at the expense of older ones. This is not true and the low-carbon economy will not rise from the ashes of energy-intensive sectors. It is also misguided to expect the national economy to survive a period without either new or existing sectors.

- Overall, the government appears to want to square the circle of supporting industries while penalising them by simply ignoring the true impact of energy prices on them.

Current cost of climate change policies

The current cost to an average chemical company implementing all existing climate-change policies is just over £1m per annum, but by 2020 the cost will rise to almost £7m. Higher costs cannot be easily passed to consumers due to tight international competition so companies' profit margins are undermined. This will cause some firms to relocate to other countries with less draconian business environments. Others will go bankrupt. Major cost influencing factors include:

- The cumulative energy-related policies of the last decade have built up an overwhelming number of costs for the industry to bear, and this is yet to be appreciated by the government. No individual cost will drive the industry out of the UK, but the overall burden will.
- Unilateral British levies. Regardless of what other countries are or aren't doing, the UK is pricing itself out of the market. The carbon price floor will be ruinous: experts claim any CO_2 permit

cost over €30/t (£27 approximately) will make UK chemical production unviable. The plans announced in the March 2011 Budget will set a minimum cost of £30 by 2020 and £70 by 2030, far over this cut-off.

- The EU's climate-change policies should create an equal burden on all member states but many choose to selectively implement the regulations or fail to meet their demands. Meanwhile, Britain 'gold plates' the regulations and implements them beyond any other country.

- Regulations have become rigid, expensive to implement and slow to take innovations into account.

The British chemical industry is up against rising international competition

There is a growing international view that Britain is losing its industrial ability and UK investments are risky. In part, this is because many other countries are happy to offer incentives to companies to establish there. Frequently, a percentage of the initial investment or export infrastructure is paid for by the state. In addition, some countries such as Egypt and Saudi Arabia offer cheap long-term energy contracts to companies below the market-rate and this saving is passed on to the consumer, undercutting the prices of UK chemicals. The government should be aware that while Brazil, Russia, India and China (the BRIC nations) are developing their chemical industries and energy efficiency, this is without concern for emissions.

There is a need for awareness of wider factors

Downstream industries reliant on chemicals are at risk of collapse if the chemical industry emigrates. Given how wide-ranging these are, from soap to silicon chip manufacturers, their additional loss would be significant. In specialised chemicals and pharmaceuticals, four jobs are reliant on every directly employed worker and for general chemicals, ten indirect jobs are at risk for each directly employed chemical worker.

Seventy per cent of Chemical Industry Association (CIA) member companies are foreign-owned and the UK is increasingly viewed internationally as a difficult place to do business. If costs rise too far, multinationals will close UK plants and move production to more welcoming countries. One multinational recently used its British workforce to construct a new plant in Portugal prior to laying them off. Foreign investment in British chemical plants is already declining, undermining the long-term viability of the sector.

There is a looming skills shortage and little sympathy for the industry. The average age of chemical workers is 50. If the sector is to grow, more graduates and vocational workers need to be enticed in. This is being held back by a lack of public awareness of how the sector has modernised and the continuation of heavy industry myths via the media.

Consequences of the chemical industry's collapse

If the government presses ahead with its current plans, it will not only be committing economic suicide, but smothering the low-carbon economy at birth. A major source of tax revenue would be lost and large numbers of newly unemployed would create a large burden on the state. Certain regions with chemical-reliant economies such as Teesside will be hit hardest at a time when the government claims to want to help these areas.

Low-carbon products will become more expensive, reducing demand for them among consumers. In addition, as industrial users disappear, the demand for energy-efficient means of production will decline, reducing the desirability of the UK as a centre of low-carbon innovations. There's no point trying to be green if the industry will just emigrate: carbon leakage will occur as chemical companies relocate to countries without proper emission controls, increasing overall global GHG levels.

Policy Recommendations:

Reassess what green targets the UK should aim for

Britain produces just two per cent of global emissions, so even becoming carbon-neutral would have little overall effect. If the government wants the UK to be a global leader on climate-change, it should be via producing the innovative products necessary to help the world reduce its emissions.

This means the chemical industry should be at the heart of any climate-change policy. Incentives on a par with other countries should be offered to chemical firms to entice them to set up in the UK. Britain should become a world-class centre for low-carbon technological products and research.

Recognise the economic reality

A balance must be struck between encouraging firms to reduce their emissions and ensuring they remain in the UK. Britain needs a policy based in the reality of the present economic situation which clearly shows the value of the chemical sector. Competitive energy costs are a must for the long-term survival of the British economy.

Long-term climate-change policies

The government must design longer-term policies that allow companies the time to adjust to emission targets and budget with the confidence that costs won't rise further. The seeds of tomorrow's low carbon future are already in existence today and a healthy chemical industry will take Britain much further than the blunt instrument of raising energy costs ever can. If the government nurtured the industry, the emissions saving ratio would double to 4:1.

Restore equality with Europe

Britain needs to push for equality of implementation at an EU-level. Countries should not be allowed to fall behind on their green targets without real penalties. At the same time, the UK should not gold-plate EU targets. The carbon price floor is in real danger of doing this.

New awareness

Ignorance of what the chemical sector does has led to the punitive cost regime. A new understanding of its economic and environmental contributions is necessary. The government and civil service need to include more industry specialists in their ranks.

Introduction

If the government presses ahead with plans to raise the cost of energy directly and indirectly to reduce carbon emissions, this will be highly damaging to many sectors of the UK economy. Those most affected will be primary manufacturers, the majority of whom require large amounts of power to run their production processes. Of these, there are some energy-intensive sectors who will really suffer: the chemicals, glass, aluminium and paper industries are just some who will be hard-pressed to maintain production in the UK if energy prices continue to be artificially increased.

In this report, the chemical industry has been singled out as an example worthy of special mention. This is because it has a dual identity. On the one hand, it *is* energy-intensive and a source of greenhouse gas emissions. Many climate change activists would be content to see it disappear from the UK on this basis. On the other hand, the chemicals sector is a large source of employment and trade income. It also produces the products and technologies vital to reducing our fossil fuel dependency, increasing energy efficiency and developing the wider low-carbon economy, all things the government wants to encourage. An examination of the chemical industry therefore reveals that by increasing the extent of climate change charges, the government will thereby undermine its own objectives as well as the national economy.

The context of existing climate change policies

The framework of policies within which the chemicals sector and all manufacturing must work is highly complex. Without an understanding of it though, it is very hard to see just how damaging these policies are, or why the cost of energy is so intimately reliant on them.

- Foremost of these policies is the 2008 Climate Change Act (CCA). This was designed to demonstrate the UK's international leadership in tackling climate-change and to help the transition to the low-carbon economy.

1

It declared a reduction in greenhouse gas (GHG) emissions of 80 per cent by 2050. More pressingly, it also decreed a GHG reduction of 34 per cent by 2020, the deepest cuts of any industrialised nation. Both of these targets are measured against a 1990 baseline. The emission cuts legally required by 2020 are 14 per cent higher than the EU's own target of at least 20 per cent by that date.

The CCA also required the creation of 'carbon budgets', which would set a level of decreasing carbon emissions over five-year periods. In May 2009, three periods were drawn up, 2008-12, 2013-17 and 2018-23. These have reductions on 1990 levels of 22 per cent, 28 per cent and 34 per cent respectively.[1]

- Britain has also signed up to the EU Renewable Energy Directive. This requires 15 per cent of British energy to be delivered from renewable sources by 2020. As the Department for Energy and Climate Change's (DECC) own website states: 'This target is equivalent to a seven-fold increase in UK renewable energy consumption from 2008 levels: the most challenging of any EU Member State.'[2]

The average 'net benefit' of the four scenarios DECC created to meet this target is -£56.75 billion by 2030.[3] There is a general consensus that the target will not be met on time.[4]

In addition to these, there are three other important policies:

- The Renewables Obligation (RO) is designed to incentivise the generation of electricity from eligible renewable sources and it obliges electricity suppliers to source a percentage of their electricity from these. At present and until 31 March 2011, 11.1 per cent must come from renewable sources. Put simply, for every megawatt hour (MWh) generated through renewables, a certificate is given to the supplier, known as a Renewable Obligation Certificate (ROC).[5] If the supplier does not have enough ROCs to cover the required percentage of output, they can pay a 'buy-out' price. This currently stands at £36.99 per MWh.[6]

It is important to note that the cost of ROCs is effectively paid by the electricity consumer, as the supplier includes the charge in their tariffs, thereby passing it on.

- The EU's Emissions Trading System (EU ETS), formerly known as the EU Emissions Trading Scheme, is a 'cap and trade' system that started in 2005. It was originally introduced as one of the key policies to help the EU meet its GHG reduction of eight per cent under the Kyoto Protocol for 2008-12.

  It affects all large emitters of CO_2, which includes energy-intensive industries such as chemicals, as well as power generators. Under the scheme, each EU member state creates a national allocation plan which is then approved by the European Commission. Then, each country allocates the allowances to its industries. At the end of each year, installations have to declare how much of their allowance they have used. If some are left, they can be sold on the market to others who emitted more than their allowances permitted. The overall level of pollution allowed is therefore pre-defined and reduced over time by reducing allowances.

  The EU ETS is now in its second phase, which widened its scope and shrank the cap. Phase III will begin in 2013 and in this, the number of free permits will fall drastically, available only to selected companies. In addition, permits will then be auctioned, which will push up the cost of electricity generated from fossil fuels substantially.

- The Climate Change Levy (CCL) is a tax on energy in all non-domestic sectors with the aim of reducing energy consumption and thereby CO_2 emissions. There are exclusions to the charge, such as on electricity generated from renewables. Energy-intensive sectors such as chemicals can receive an 80 per cent reduction provided they subscribe to a specific climate change agreement.

  Nuclear power is not exempt from the levy, despite the fact it generates no carbon emissions through power generation. The CCL therefore appears to confuse energy-intensity and carbon-

3

intensity, seeing the former leading to the latter, which is not always the case. In reality, it can be seen as primarily attempting to incentivise energy efficiency rather than GHG reduction.

It is highly likely that the carbon price floor (see p. 40), as announced in the 2011 Budget, will be introduced as part of a reform of the CCL.

The above are simplified but accurate descriptions, but are not an exhaustive list: many other small but significant charges, levies and taxes are also payable by industry. The overall density of policy and regulation means that it is very hard to quantify the effect all the climate change legislation. Recent figures from July 2010 put the overall increase in energy bills by 2020 (taking electricity, gas and emission reducing schemes together) at 18 per cent to 141 per cent of current costs.[7] This is a huge variable and the lack of clarity is almost as damaging to industry as the potential price rises.

It should also be noted that Britain cannot escape the EU targets or taxes it has signed up to. We must therefore aim for the 15 per cent renewables goal, even though it is highly damaging economically and unlikely to be reached within the specified timeframe. The only real way out of this would be to leave the EU, an unlikely scenario. However, national legislation such as the CCL can be revoked. In sum, while there is a substantial basic level of environmental polices Britain must enact, we are going much farther than this. The UK is aiming for a 34 per cent reduction in emissions by 2020 instead of 20 per cent like the rest of the EU, and this burden will be felt in energy prices and emission taxes unique to the UK.

The UK chemical industry's place in the economy

Contrary to popular opinion, industrial activity in the UK is certainly not dead or dying. Before the recession, British manufacturing as a whole had been growing in terms of output for decades.[8] Using constant 2006 prices, in 2009, manufacturing contributed £132.2 billion gross value added to the economy while financial intermediation accounted for 'only' £97.6 billion. The chemical industry is one of the foremost manufacturing sectors, and has experienced something of a renaissance in recent years, as the following points explain:

- **Position within manufacturing:** The chemical industry is one of the principle contributors to the economy, both in terms of employing a vast workforce and generating income. Figure 1 (p. 79) shows the steady rise in its importance within the context of the five other largest manufacturing sectors. It rose from the sixth largest contributor to the UK economy to the third in only 17 years, with a gross value added contribution of £17.1 billion in 2009 at 2006 prices. Crucially, this has been due to the increase in chemical output rather than the decline in other sectors. During the recession, the chemical industry also suffered the second smallest decline in production. Figure 1's numbers are not distorted by inflation.

- **Workforce:** This development of the chemical industry over the last decade has mostly occurred under the radar of the government and national press; hence while many know manufacturing is resurging, they do not realise the chemicals sector is a protagonist in this. Figure 2 (p. 80) shows the fall in the sector's direct workforce in recent years. Due to the nature of Office for National Statistic methods, this figure underestimates the number of actual chemical workers, which the Chemical Industry Association estimates at 200,000.

However, as actual employment has declined, productivity has risen. This is a result of the industry's shift from dirty, labour-intensive production to capital intensive, efficient and automated production relying on minimal human intervention. It has moved away from large, mostly unskilled staffs towards smaller but highly-skilled ones composed primarily of science, technology, engineering and maths (STEM) graduates.

As seen in Figure 3 (p. 81), the combination of advanced processes and quality workers has meant that output per worker has risen, a trend that has accelerated in recent years. The shedding of employees has led politicians to assume falsely the chemicals sector has declined and is no longer integral to the British economy. This is not the case.

- **Positive trade balance:** The UK's overall current balance of trade in goods is negative to the tune of -£97.2 billion, a record high, but would be much worse were it not for the chemicals sector, which accounts for 15 per cent of goods exported by UK companies.[9] Moreover it contributes positively to the British balance of trade, a unique trait among all the manufacturing sectors. Figure 4 (p. 82) shows that this has always been the case since 1999, and it has been performing remarkably better than the other four largest sectors, all of which produce large volumes of goods but overall suffer from far more imports than exports.

  In 2009, the chemical trade balance amounted to almost a £9 billion surplus and this has been increasing steadily since 2007. In comparison, the food and drink industry contributed a deficit of almost £14 billion. Indeed, the chemical industry contributes £30 million a day to the UK's balance of trade while the rest of manufacturing amounts to a £300 million daily loss.[10]

- **Wider value of chemical related industries:** On its own, the economic weight of the chemicals sector is a substantial £60 billion, but when all the other industries that the chemical products feed into are also counted, this figure rises dramatically. A report commissioned by the Royal Society of Chemistry found that chemistry-reliant industries contributed £258 billion value-added to the UK economy in 2007, equivalent to 21 per cent per cent of UK GDP.[11] While not all this value can be sourced back to the chemicals sector, a significant part would be lost were it not the chemical industry.

Despite all this, the chemical industry is still relatively unknown and outsiders have often paid little attention to its worth and contribution to the UK economy. INEOS, with an annual turnover of over $28 billion, is probably the largest British company that almost no one has heard of.

Cluster case study: NEPIC

The North East of England Process Industry Cluster (NEPIC) is one of the organisations at the heart of Britain's successful chemical industry. While the term 'process' includes non-chemicals sectors such as biotechnology, almost all the firms within the group are reliant on chemicals for their production, the majority of which are produced by other firms within the cluster. In total, NEPIC, based in Teesside and the surrounding area, represents over 500 companies, 70 per cent of these being SMEs, which employ 40,000 directly in the processes industries and a further 280,000 employed in downstream jobs, ranging from logistical transporters to analysts and marketers. NEPIC has already helped generate over £1 billion for the sector over a six-year period and the cluster has delivered £4.5 billion of exports. This is set to increase, with NEPIC activity having gained £4.6 billion in investments to date. The simplest issues most commonly associated with cluster management such as ignorance about neighbouring companies' products have been eliminated. Dr Stan Higgins, the Chief Executive of NEPIC, said:

> We wanted to keep value here rather than elsewhere. Five years ago a company from Newcastle was making steel tablet moulds and came to me saying 'a German company has me make this, send it to Germany, puts on a German quality paper then sends it back up the road and charges them five times more'. We're talking about factories within two miles of each other—they just weren't talking to each other.

The strength of NEPIC and its chemical industry has been refusal to rest on its laurels and its success has been due to the acknowledgement that it is reliant on more than just networking opportunities. Unlike most other self-defined clusters, NEPIC was set up with the specific aim of fostering growth in the region, not just improving conditions for existing companies. It is currently hoping to channel a further £8 billion of investment in new companies that will utilise the existing products and resources available in the region. In addition, over 120 executives of NEPIC-based companies use a small amount of their time to share information, pursue the issues facing the cluster and track down investors. The cluster also has also benefitted from the ICI legacy, which has provided the Wilton Centre, where solid research facilities allow engagement in large amounts of research and development (R&D). When industrial processes are being scaled up, these can be carried out onsite at the Wilton Centre where NEPIC has its headquarters, and once spin-off companies develop, there are many open sites to settle on in the area. The success of the NE region is in part also due to the economies of scale it offers. The sites in the North East are often huge and involve large logistical exercises. Europe's biggest bioethanol plant is situated in Wilton, Teesside and receives 40 tonnes of wheat every five minutes. Without the ability to lower the cost-base by producing ethanol *en masse*, the profitably of the enterprise would be minimal.

Company case study: Lucite International

Lucite is located within the NEPIC area and produces methyl methacrylate (MMA), a raw material in plastics and paint production. Its primary market is overseas and the company relies on exports for the bulk of its revenue. While it has few downstream companies within the NEPIC cluster, Lucite is reliant on upstream integration such as purchasing ammonia from the nearby GrowHow plant (see p. 26).

Lucite's plant is one of the largest in the world and its competitive advantage relies on this. The size allows production of MMA in bulk and at a low cost via an economy of scale. So far, Lucite has managed to maintain this advantage and used to it overcome the other cost burdens UK production brings with it, but as energy and regulatory costs rise, this advantage is being eroded.

NEPIC has been planning for the future and for the low-carbon economy by winning investment in areas such as biofuel and renewables, sectors that rely on chemicals for their development. As these develop, so too will the need for investment in the nearby chemical companies that supply their raw materials. NEPIC embraces these chemical firms as part of the low-carbon economy and an integral foundation for its success, rather than perceiving them as a negative high-carbon burden as some politicians do. This integration has meant the cluster developed so that all its processes are interlinked and, rather than creating a direct up-down supply chain, a web of industry has been created with chemicals as an integral element. While this means that the loss of individual companies does not lead to a domino effect of downstream firms also collapsing, the emigration of chemical firms would have a disastrous effect on a wide range of NEPIC's processes, hurting the national economy as a whole.

Trade bodies and pharmaceuticals

NEPIC deals with the North East, but there are other trade bodies that cover the whole of the UK. They also have the specialised knowledge required to help and lobby on behalf of the chemicals sector in a manner that the Department for Business, Innovation and Skills (BIS) cannot. The Chemical Industry Association (CIA) is the principal industry body for chemical and pharmaceutical producers. Other pharmaceutical trade bodies exist to deal with the 'medical' side of that sector, while the CIA focuses on the manufacturing side. Their membership reflects this and includes pharmaceutical companies that still make their products in the UK, such as GlaxoSmithKline. Other businesses have joined the CIA to keep abreast of the developments that affect their chemical suppliers. In total, it has around 140 members, 70 per cent of which are foreign-owned firms, but it also comprises smaller members who face the same issues as SMEs. The CIA provides advice and services to its members but also deals with influencing the policy agenda and regulatory aspects of the chemical industry.

The Energy Intensive Users Group is a similar organisation which primarily campaigns for more competitive energy costs, arguing that this is the source of many sectors' competitive edge. As shall be seen, this is certainly the case for the chemicals sector, which is very energy-intensive and forms a core part of the Group's membership.

Within the UK, pharmaceutical production is an important sub-sector of the chemical industry. In recent years, however, this industry has moved away from actually producing the proverbial 'little white pill' in Britain as these can be produced cheaper elsewhere. Instead, the UK pharmaceutical industry now focuses on R&D and testing. This is augmented by the fact that the UK has skilled companies able to develop pilot plants and ultimately scale-up to commercial production. This is where Britain retains a strong competitive advantage through focusing on high quality advanced manufacturing, a trait representative of wider UK chemical production. According to the CIA, some companies have returned their production of active chemical ingredients to the UK after finding that in India and China the quality was not sufficiently and reliably high.

Pfizer

The recent decision of pharmaceuticals giant Pfizer to close its Kent R&D facility should act as a wake-up call for the Government that all is not well within the pharmaceutical sector. The loss of Pfizer from the UK is a significant blow to the economy, especially since up to 2,400 are being made redundant in the process. The company had invested £329 million in its UK research facilities in 2009.

According to an ex-Pfizer employee, the loss of positive incentives associated with ROCs meant the scheme became purely punitive and a cost that only had to be paid in the UK. This meant the motivation to invest in British facilities was lost and, as other advantages were also eroded, the Renewables Obligation played a significant part in the decision to relocate.

Britain has a vested interest in ensuring domestic retention of both intellectual property and the R&D element of the pharmaceutical sector. According to Fiona Ferguson, Media and Government Relations Manager at the Chemical Industry Association, the crucial issue is that: 'the supply chains in the chemical industry are highly integrated, to lose one element of the chain such as pharmaceuticals would impact businesses that sell products to a wide variety of supply chains as each loss of revenue stream chips away at their long term viability'. The recognition of downstream industries is crucial to assessing the real value of the chemicals sector and pharmaceuticals are an integral part of this.

The chemical industry and energy usage

Energy prices are for the most part the largest cost facing chemical firms, constituting between 30 per cent and 70 per cent of their expenditure. Many of the basic chemical manufacturers have to use a vast amount of energy in their processes: according to INEOS Chlor, their Runcorn plant uses as much electricity as a city the size of Liverpool.[12]

This has led to accusations that the chemical industry is energy greedy, wasteful and unproductive. This is not the case. The manufacture of chemicals is subject to the laws of thermodynamics and high energy levels are frequently required by default and unavoidable. However, relative energy efficiency fundamentally underpins the competitiveness of the industry's business model—the reality is that whilst the UK chemicals sector is energy-intensive, it also strives to be energy-efficient.

It is in the interests of any chemical company to keep its energy costs to a minimum in order to maximise its profit margin. Energy costs constitute the largest proportion of its overheads, so there is every incentive to keep these as low as possible to maintain a

> *It is in the interests of any chemical company to keep its energy costs to a minimum in order to maximise its profit margin.*

competitive edge. Hence, even if there were no energy-related taxes and regulations, if chemicals manufacturers could consume less, they would. As the necessary technology is being developed, the industry is implementing it. However, the mentality behind current government policies assumes that the industry lacks this independent will to reduce its energy consumption, and that it therefore needs more penalties than incentives.

In terms of greenhouse gas reduction, using Department for Energy and Climate Change (DECC) statistics, the disappearance of the chemicals sector would directly save on average 10.79 million metric tonnes of CO_2 equivalent (Mt CO_2e) out of a total of UK generation of 627.85 Mt CO_2e. Even out of the total industrial output of 275.74 Mt CO_2e, the chemicals sector is only responsible for 3.9 per cent of energy related emissions.[13] Indirectly, the sector is responsible for power generation emissions, but the total sum is not large enough to justify penalising the industry out of existence when considering the carbon-saving products it delivers as well.

The current government's plans

The government has published two major documents to date that detail its current strategy for the economy. Both entitled 'Growth Review', the first, published last November, mapped out plans for the whole economy; while the second, from December, focused on manufacturing.[14] Both declared renewed governmental support for rebalancing the economy and highlighted the importance of manufacturing in achieving this. They both also singled out the chemical industry as a special sector to be encouraged, and promised a myriad of funds and incentives for its development.[15] The wider Review stated: 'the government is making trade, export promotion and attracting investment to the UK one of its priorities'. This too is a laudable aim that would boost the central contribution of the chemical industry to the national economy.[16]

The Reviews sound reassuring, but contain an inherent contradiction which will serve to undermine commitment to the chemicals sector and, in all likeliness, its future in the UK. Alongside assurances that business costs will be kept down and competitive edges maintained, the November Review declares: 'the government has committed to reform the electricity market, including supporting the carbon price in the UK to encourage more low-carbon generation'.[17] The overall aim is not industrial support but 'ensuring that the UK is well-positioned for the transition to a low-carbon economy'.[18]

The assumption here and more widely in government rhetoric is that Britain's low-carbon economy (LCE) can only be created through pricing high-carbon energy out of the market. This idea is an inherited legacy from the previous Labour administration and has so far remained unquestioned. It is presumed that the LCE is one in which as little energy as possible is used and fossil fuels are replaced by renewable sources of energy. This is only half the picture: in the short and medium-term, the LCE is about utilising energy as efficiently as possible and operating a mixed range of renewable and non-renewable fuel sources. The full substitution of fossil fuels can only be a long-term goal as it relies on technology still being developed.

> *The full substitution of fossil fuels can only be a long-term goal as it relies on technology still being developed.*

The government's policies therefore pull in two opposing directions. It believes it can support the growth of the chemical industry while also attacking its Achilles' heel—its high energy usage. The promise of the 'greenest government ever' has led to many proposals that will damage the sector, despite the December *Growth Review* recognising that high energy prices are a 'barrier to advanced manufacturing growth'. It stated that many manufacturers 'are within or closely related to energy-intensive industries that depend on manageable energy costs and security of supply to remain globally competitive'.[19]

This is very true for the chemical industry. The production of chemicals requires a large quantity of energy, not just to fuel the power-hungry plants, but in some cases because gas or electricity is directly used in the production process as a raw material. Many working in chemicals feel escalating energy costs are the principal issue that will make or break the entire £60 billion

> *The government is actively working against the British chemical industry.*

13

sector. Just offering other tax breaks and other minor perks, as both *Reviews* recommend, will not be enough to offset this. Over 600,000 jobs are at risk if the government continues to declare that its current model for creating the LCE is the only possible method.

The aim of this paper is not to pressure the government to provide subsidies and grants for the chemicals sector to keep it in this country. Instead, the purpose is to highlight that by leading the world on punative climate change policies, the government is doing exactly the opposite and actively working against the British chemical industry.

1

The Past: The Consequences
of Existing Policies

At a basic level, the government's decision to raise the cost of energy through levies and taxes has put a strain on many firms that are now struggling to survive in the UK and face being pushed out of the market. As the price of their main overhead rises, they either have to risk lower demand by raising the cost of their product or absorb the blow in their profit margin. Large chemical multinationals, with the luxury of being able to relocate their plants, will channel their investments elsewhere. Phil Bailey, the Cassel site director at Lucite International, said: 'energy is an issue in the UK, relative to some locations, and moreover energy legislation in particular is a growing issue for us, again relative to other locations where you could manufacture'. The deliberate raising of energy costs is a long-term problem and, in addition, their frequent modification means that there is little certainly as to what the future burden of these will be. This means that companies are unable to really budget for the future and draw up a long-term strategy to cope with rising prices.

The danger of rapidly rising costs

The government's myriad of levies and taxes are aimed at encouraging reduced energy consumption and greater energy generation from renewable sources. Given that the energy-intensive sector is consuming so much energy, the passed-on cost falls on them heavily, and each small price-rise can have a magnified effect on

> There is the potential, in less than two years, for the entire sector to be priced out the market in the UK.

their profit margins. The effect of the costs introduced so far will increase rapidly in the coming years, as shown in Figure 5 (p. 83).

15

Combined with the rising energy costs also shown in Figure 5, which are pushed up by various extra charges as well, bills will become highly burdensome. This comes from an independent investigation by Waters Wye Associates, a consultancy firm. Similarly, Figure 6 (p. 84) displays the predicted climate-change costs for a UK chemical firm that wished to remain anonymous, showing that even discounting energy prices, the base costs for production will still increase significantly. Both figures demonstrate that while energy costs as of 2010-12 are comparatively small and increasing slowly, by 2013 they will start to increase rapidly. This would go some way to explaining why the looming problem has not been seen as a major concern by the government, but it is critical to realise that there is the potential, in less than two years, for the entire sector to be priced out the market in the UK, let alone the costs that will be incurred by 2020.

The Renewable Heat Incentive

The contribution of energy-intensive companies to the Renewable Heat Incentive (RHI) was altered in the October 2010 Spending Review to avoid burdening the firms with unsustainable bills. It was expected that by 2020, they would be paying an additional £2 million per annum. This U-turn was a good thing and highly valued by manufacturers as breathing space among the other regulations that have to be implemented as well.

However, the relief given by altering the RHI has the potential to be negated. The proposed carbon floor price (see p. 40), which was announced two months later in December 2010, will have a similarly devastating effect when it comes into force. As a consequence, Lisa Waters, a director of Waters Wye, suggested: 'the risk is still there, but the companies do not know the scale. The Government has seriously underestimated the cost of the carbon floor price... you can't see how this will not push up the price of electricity.'

According to Deborah Pritchard Jones, the Business Projects & Public Affairs manager at GrowHow, a British producer of fertiliser, there was a need for independent analysis of energy costs: 'when BIS do their impact assessments, they use a business user, basically a supermarket, not an energy-intensive manufacturer, so we wanted to construct an average energy-intensive user'. The use of low-energy-using businesses in such assessments led Chris Huhne, the Secretary of State for Energy and Climate Change, to state that:

> all studies on so-called carbon leakage [the emigration of industries abroad], whether they were done for the EU or the studies we have commissioned between BIS and DECC actually suggest a very marginal effect'.[1]

This conclusion is unsurprising when low-energy users are involved and it would appear that the government is therefore ignorant of the effect its policies are having. However, this is also a convenient outcome for those wanting to suggest that raising the cost of energy will not matter to businesses. The output of these official assessments fails to accurately reflect the likely outcome that current energy policies will have on the energy-intensive sectors and do not bear resemblance to the reality of the situation.

The Waters Wye Associates investigation found that the government's current policies will cause the cost of energy to rise — dramatically so in the long-term. Past events have already shown what the consequences of price spikes are. Fiona Ferguson said:

> Last winter we had a cold spot when companies just had to close down because cost was too high. Others shut down production temporarily, but when you're talking about big companies which can switch production to other countries, you're worried that they may never come back.

Price spikes reveal the vulnerability of British industry, but while they are a temporary phenomenon, the problem now facing the industry is a permanent, long-term one.

As the cost of energy is forced to rise, this issue will only get worse, and for a company such as Lucite, which has similar production costs compared to its international rivals, the effect of rising energy costs could be the difference between continued UK production and emigration. Phil Bailey explained:

> Energy costs as a differentiator are quite significant. The basic commodities that go to make up the product are relatively similar, whether you buy them in the UK, in Europe, in China or the USA, so energy costs are a bit you can actually influence. It's several million pounds off the bottom line and we don't have much chance of recovering that through our customers if our competitors aren't seeing it as well. It's a big hit to our profitability.

The danger of cumulative costs

The problem with the current green levies and energy taxes is not so much the effect of each one, but their cumulative effect. The chemical industry could cope with any of the energy-cost burdens the government and EU want to impose—if they were applied in isolation without any others. Indeed, a single cost would be a sound balance between nurturing the sector for its long-term potential and encouraging it to lower its carbon emissions in the meantime. However, the current regime creates an environment that over-burdens the sector. Jeremy Nicholson, the Director of the Energy Intensive Users Group argued: 'the idea that you can burden highly trade-exposed sectors to fundamentally uncompetitive energy prices *ad infinitum* without it causing large economic damage is absurd'.

The policy regime will lead to a 'straw that broke the camel's back' scenario where the cumulative effect, rather than any individual levy, will cause the collapse of the UK chemicals sector. The uncertainty and confusion over costs not only hinders the direct chemical producers, but also prevents investment. Phil Bailey argued:

> You can't pin it on one particular thing... but you start to question doing the investment—at the moment we are investing a lot of money in increasing capacity and reducing costs and as soon as you stop doing that then it all snowballs and you start to become less competitive and the impact of it becomes larger relatively. You could see this happening in 2013-4 where you question if it's worth doing the next £5 million investment when you could be paying £15 million from energy legislation in 10 years' time.

New charges are still being added to the already substantial list of costs that the chemical industry pays. This is a result of shifting the bill for renewable power generation away from the state, and officially towards the power generator though in actuality it is lumped on the end user. The electricity consumer is already paying for this through the Renewables Obligation and Chris Huhne has stated that he wants this to continue: 'we will do the same [as the EU ETS] with our own electricity markets reform, putting in place the institutional mechanisms to deliver what OFGEM estimates as £200 billion of low-carbon investment'.[2]

The disproportionate burden on SMEs

The companies worst hit by cumulative rising costs will be the SMEs that now make up the vast majority of UK chemical manufacturers, and Table 1 shows just how many there are within the industry. The *Growth Reviews* and many governmental speeches since have placed strong emphasis on creating better business conditions for SMEs. Climate-change legislation is having a contrary effect.

While the higher prices are a general burden, SMEs are often left confused by the overly complicated levies and when they are exempt from these. Bigger companies normally have dedicated staff members hired to deal with these, but SMEs rarely do. Instead, responsibility frequently falls to the boss of the company whose time and effort could be better spent on positive activities. Looking at Table 1, it is clear that when considering economic growth and the chemical industry, the Government needs to keep the requirements and vulnerability of SMEs at the forefront of its mind.

Huhne's commitment to charging energy-intensive sectors for the privilege of existing in Britain can be seen in the new bill for energy transmission developments being footed by businesses, in addition to their existing RO levy. The new focus on offshore power generation requires the National Grid to be upgraded with highly expensive cables, not only to connect the Grid to the wind turbines, but also elsewhere to accommodate them coming on-stream. Jeremy Nicholson has calculated that the overall cost of all this for energy-intensive sectors will be £15-£20 billion. He predicted the cumulative effect of these additional charges: 'it's entirely possible that the cost... of subsidising energy renewables will be at least as significant in terms of the impact on power prices by 2020 as the EU ETS'. Energy-intensive industries have yet to be consulted on trans-mission costs. Given the review of these will take roughly a year-and-a-half to complete, there is ample time for the sectors to be consulted on whether and how they can bear the cost without their competitive edge being undermined.

Table 1: Number of UK chemical firms by size in 2010

Employees	0-4	5-9	10-19	20-49	50-99	100-249	250-499
Number of firms	1,325	480	380	440	235	160	60

Source: ONS, UK Business Size Statistics, Table A2.1

Over-regulation

No one within the chemicals industry thinks that it should be deregulated. Fiona Ferguson said:

> The chemical industry is high hazard but it is increasingly low risk. This is in part because good health, safety and environmental performance makes good economic sense but it is also because of regulation. The frustration is often with the complexity, inflexibility and unnecessary costs and shifting goal posts. Frequently there is a problem with guidance arriving extremely close to the deadline for implementation which does not help businesses plan.

However, there are currently too many policies aimed at tackling climate change. This has led to the danger of cumulative costs when what is really required is a simplification of charges, exemptions and targets. The government itself has acknowledged the need to streamline the regulation: 'Government aims to begin shortly a public dialogue with participants on proposals to simplify the scheme' (the Carbon Reduction Commitment).[3]

The volume of red tape is the consequence of regulation being created by civil servants who have no real understanding of how the chemical industry works or what it can cope with. Stan Higgins said:

> The amount of detail we sometimes put into our regulation means that it gets interpreted by civil servants in a rigorous way that then becomes so rigid that actually the real industry can't find its way through it... the regulations become a cage.

The CRC

The Carbon Reduction Commitment Energy Efficiency Scheme (CRC) was created in 2010 as a 'cap and trade' scheme and it aims to cut carbon emissions by 1.2 million tonnes by 2020. It currently charges £12 per tonne of CO_2, but from April 2013 permits will be auctioned.

Those companies covered by the EU ETS and climate change agreements are exempt. In other words, the CRC is aimed at large non-energy intensive firms and the majority of chemical firms are exempt and unaffected. In theory.

Policies have become something of a quagmire and dissuade businesses from moving to or continuing production in the UK. The CIA had hoped the CRC would improve matters and, according to Fiona Ferguson, expected it to be 'part of a programme to simplify all of them [green taxes], so it might not be so bad... Most of our members can opt out of the CRC thanks to Climate Change Agreements but the process is not a simple one.' However, all companies were forced to register for CRC anyway, pay an admin fee and provide various company data before they could opt out by citing membership of one of the schemes granting exemption. The difficulty of withdrawing reflects the current policy ethos that companies are 'guilty until proven innocent'.

Moreover, the CRC has lost its way in the wake of the October 2010 Spending Review. It was originally engineered to provide rebates to those companies that have the largest reduction in their emissions while charging the worst performers in full. As such the money it gained was redistributed to the best performers and encouraged carbon-saving measures. However, the rebates incentive has been scrapped so the CRC is now punitive regardless of whether businesses reduce their emissions. With £1 billion already raised through the CRC, many businesses had expected to see their money returned to them in due course and budgeted accordingly. This revenue has now been pocketed by the state, ignoring the needs and concerns of industry and future costs will soar, as estimated by PriceWaterhouseCoopers. It found that the changes will cost an extra £76,000 per year in the first year, rising to £114,000 per year by 2015, for a business with an average £1m gas and electricity bill.[4]

Overregulation at an EU level

Some EU directives are far too sweeping and generalised, failing to take individual circumstances into account. This has created some unique challenges for UK companies.

For example, one British chemical company has a plant on the coast and uses sea water as a coolant in its processes before cleaning the water and pumping it back into the Irish Sea. The Industrial Emissions Directive was originally worded so that all chemical plants must desalinate used water prior to releasing it, on the assumption all plants used river water which therefore did need desalination. For the sea water-using British firm, this would have been a pointless and expensive task.

It was only after industry wide protests that the EU made the amendment and acknowledged local circumstances. While the situation ended with a satisfactory conclusion, industry time and resources were wasted while the difficulty of manufacturing in Britain (and Europe) became apparent.

In addition, changes to regulation are often implemented too quickly, not allowing for an adequate transition period that would give companies the chance to adjust to new costs. By continually raising targets, something the EU is guilty of, too great a reduction is then expected within too short a timeframe. The continual addition of regulations and levies means the phasing system of older legislation is being undermined. For example, the EU ETS will only come into full force with Phase III in 2013 and this had been decided eight years in advance, giving companies room for manoeuvre. Since then other hard-hitting plans have been introduced and there is no certainty that further chargers will not be implemented on top of these too.

REACH

The greatest of the non-energy related EU regulations to have an effect on the chemicals sector is the Registration, Evaluation and Authorisation and Restriction of Chemicals (REACH). It's aims are:

- In its own words: 'to ensure a high level of protection of human health and the environment from the risks that can be posed by chemicals... enhance levels of competition and innovation'.[5]

- Once it has come into full force, REACH will require all chemicals produced in Europe in quantities of over one tonne per annum to be registered with the European Chemical Agency. This registration will involve creating safety information and analysing the chemicals to evaluate if they are harmful to humans.

- Under REACH requirements, the first registration deadline was 30 November 2010 and required all companies in the EU to register chemicals they produce in quantities of over 1,000 tonnes a year as well as any hazardous ones. For GrowHow, the cost was €306,000 for their primary registration.

- Once registered, companies will then be assessed by the European Chemicals Agency and a more thorough evaluation may be made if deemed necessary.

- The outcome may be full permission to continue producing a certain chemical, denial of a production license or production being allowed only for a specific purpose or length of time. This means that the future of many chemicals is uncertain, which is not a situation suited to investment.

While many in the chemical industry agree with the principle of REACH, they feel that the EU has gone the wrong way about implementing it and feel that it is doing more harm than good to their businesses. This cost depends on the number of chemicals each company produces, and for the most diverse firms, the price could be huge. Ferguson recounted:

> One of our large members estimated the other day that by 2018 they will have spent €500 million complying with REACH. They felt that if REACH is properly enforced it will have been worthwhile expenditure for the good of peoples' health, the environment and for confidence in the chemical industry.

However, the guidelines were not sufficiently well defined for the industry to comply easily. For example, GrowHow produces anhydrous ammonia. It was unclear whether this was defined as a 'substance' or a 'mixture' and therefore whether it had to be registered by the 2010 deadline or the far later secondary 2015 one by which mixtures have to be registered. It was only six weeks before the 30 November deadline that GrowHow was told it had to be registered in 2010.

The EU's end-goal is to condense the 800-page report on each chemical into a one-page safety sheet for end-users. Many large chemical firms though already produce such a thing and have documented the downstream effect of their product. The principal difference is the detail and standardisation into an EU format but the production process of the official REACH sheet is overly complicated. Just how this feat of reduction will be performed is still unknown and hasn't been thought through: the huge concentration of information undermines the need for a full report in the first place.

Whilst the EU claims the regulation will improve competitiveness, REACH will do nothing of the sort. The large costs involved will have to be paid by the chemical companies themselves which Fiona Ferguson stated as 'a couple of hundred thousand euros' for registration 'and possibly a lot more in research' if further evaluation is deemed necessary. This cost might be viable for bulk-produced non-volatile chemicals, but not for very hazardous chemicals produced in small quantities. The latter are required by companies such as BAE Systems but, if not registered, or if the costs of registering and likely analysis are too high to justify production, the production of the chemical will cease and businesses will have to look outside Britain for their supply.

In addition, REACH will disproportionately affect SMEs. The time and effort required for compliance is considerable, but they rarely have anyone dedicated to deal with it. While larger companies will be able to outsource or hire a specialist to deal with the arduous registration process, most SMEs will have their compliance work done by the head of the company who has better things to be doing. In addition, many SMEs will struggle to find the spare funds available to pay for registration. This is problematic, as many new and innovative chemicals are first produced through small companies, so this is a significant barrier to entering the market.

While the hope is that all European produced chemicals will be registered by 2018, the innovation in chemical creation will not stop and new or modified ones will be developed. As this occurs there will be a continual need to register these, the cost of which will stifle R&D, especially since this cost is likely to be greater given they will be unknown and frequently require the full expensive analysis. It is perverse for the British government to accept REACH as it is, because the majority of the chemicals needed for the low-carbon economy are still being or are yet to be developed. Imposing an instant cost on the chemicals sector's potential contribution to reducing climate change is not in the interests of anyone and is a large barrier to innovation.

A further issue associated with the regulation is that importing a chemical into Europe still requires compliance with REACH. This burden though will have to be paid for by the European importer, rather than the chemical provider, meaning this is a cost extra-EU companies will avoid. Even these firms are unhappy with the regulation though, which they see as inevitably reducing the demand for their products as it limits European buyers to just those willing to register the chemical and shoulder this cost. Stan Higgins explained, 'when I was in India recently, I saw a really angry response to REACH by Indian companies who actually see it as a barrier to trade'.

Company case study: GrowHow and gas prices

GrowHow's success and willingness to reduce its emissions have gained it recognition from the government. *The Carbon Plan* of March 2011 singles it out for a case study, describing the firm as an ideal model of industry and government working in harmony.[6] There is sad irony, then, in the fact that the same government is still committed to pricing GrowHow out of existence.

GrowHow's fertiliser has been estimated to save 6.2 tonnes of carbon for every tonne emitted in its manufacture.[7] Despite this, the importance of fertiliser is not always acknowledged and Stan Higgins argued the firm is undervalued: 'why we don't see fertilisation of the earth for food growth as a leading edge technology I don't know—it is as far as I'm concerned'.

GrowHow's production relies on natural gas and it is the UK's biggest gas consumer, using it both as a feedstock and as a source of fuel. It accounts for one per cent of all British gas consumption and uses more than the cities of Manchester and Liverpool combined. This level of demand is a necessity rather than a sign of wastefulness, as gas is the most efficient means of making fertiliser and there is currently no economic low-carbon alternative. The cost of gas makes up 68 per cent of GrowHow's variable manufacturing costs so it is hugely vulnerable to increases in its price.

Background to GrowHow

GrowHow is the sole UK manufacturer of chemical fertiliser and the largest producer of ammonia and nitric acid in the country. It operates from a site in Billingham that was originally part of ICI's fertiliser division. The site was sold off and after passing through various companies, GrowHow was formed there in 2007. It is a 50:50 joint venture company owned by CF Industries and Yara International ASA.

GrowHow's ammonium nitrate fertiliser is used UK-wide for food production and has a healthy export trade. With global population increases putting increasing pressure on food supply, the market for fertilisers can only rise, and via GrowHow, the UK is well placed to take advantage of this.

GrowHow's fertiliser allowed the maximum responsible output of food while minimising soil erosion and unnecessary emissions: these products are integral to the low-carbon economy. In theory, GrowHow should be a model example of a chemical company enjoying the potential for long-term success.

GrowHow faces international competition from businesses in states such as Russia and Egypt. These countries offer a cheap fixed-cost gas supply to incentivise businesses to locate their manufacturing there. This has been giving direct rivals a boost and the ability to undercut GrowHow's prices.

The difficulty caused by high fuel prices for gas-dependent companies has already been seen. The previous gas price spike of 2005-07 caused GrowHow to be formed, from the only two fertiliser companies surviving the spike, as a means of preserving British fertiliser production. Even after its creation, as a response to what was then almost the highest gas price in the world, GrowHow had to shut down certain parts of its production for three months. This is not a simple decision: GrowHow's products are made in a continuous process that runs 24-hours every day. Unlike some other chemical companies, the plants take days to start up so they cannot easily be shut down, even when gas costs spike, as last occurred in January 2010. There is no solution to handle permanently increased gas costs.

Regardless of levies, the pressure to maintain continuous production in the face of high prices has provided a huge incentive for GrowHow to minimise its gas consumption and improve efficiency. However, while it has continued to invest in energy-efficiency measures, the cost of doing so is rising. This is because all the easy and quick innovations have been implemented, and meeting further emissions goals requires greater investment. As *The Carbon Plan* points out, between now and 2013, GrowHow is spending £35 million on their ammonia plants to reduce their emissions by 1.2 million tonnes. Commenting on the cooperation between GrowHow and DECC, Deborah Pritchard Jones said:

> GrowHow has made the investments, responded to the signals we have been given to reduce our emissions to the lowest levels, on a proactive basis. This is how the relationship should work. However, if we are put out of business as a consequence of an excessively punitive environmental taxation regime, it ceases to be a positive case study and becomes an illustration of the way in which our regime has failed.

Upgrading the plants is an incremental and expensive business: factoring in other associated costs, this means a cost of over £400 per tonne of CO_2 reduced, 'which is huge' Pritchard Jones claims, but necessary: 'we carry on doing this because the energy efficiency of our ammonia plants is what drives a fertiliser business'. It is clear that the high cost of gas is providing its own green incentives, regardless of climate-change regulations.

In recent years, gas prices have been more manageable and Pritchard Jones said: 'we have been very lucky in the sense that UK gas prices and the gas market, relative to our competition in and outside Europe, have looked better than they have for a considerable period of time'. This lower cost can therefore be passed onto the consumer, allowing GrowHow to consolidate and grow. The likelihood of this continuing though is now very reduced, due in part to the market but also to government decisions. In terms of the natural market price of gas, two major factors will likely cause a rise:

1. The recovery of energy-intensive economies like the US and the Middle East will mean a resurgence in demand for gas. This will raise production costs and with no long-term contracts on gas supply, British users will face far higher prices.

2. In addition, feedstock companies like GrowHow are now in competition with others who rely on gas indirectly via electricity generation. This has been a result of new combined cycle-gas turbines coming on stream, shifting the emphasising of power generation from coal to gas while nuclear facilities are being built.

Carbon Capture Storage (CCS)

CCS is a process where CO_2 is 'captured' when released from generators and then stored so it is not released into the atmosphere, usually in the form of injecting it deep into the Earth.

The UK is developing this new technology and DECC has asked power companies to apply for funding to trial the process. Chris Huhne hopes CCS will allow the British power sector to reduce its emissions by 80 per cent by 2030.

Originally planned just for coal power stations, the restrictions imposing this have been removed. Gas has now been included on the basis that this will be a principal source of power in years to come One gas CCS plant is now hoped for among the four CCS projects the Government has promised to deliver.

If the government adds extra charges on top of the market cost of natural gas, this will be very harmful to the industry. This can already be seen in a recent policy by the government to extend the CCS coal programme to gas, which will require up to £9 billion of funding. Just how this funding will be delivered is as yet unknown. A levy on energy costs and direct taxes have both been mooted by the Department of Energy and Climate Change as a means to raising this huge sum.[8]

The problem is that the majority of the chemical producers who rely on gas as their feedstock cannot change easily to another fuel type and so a price-hike will render them unable to continue production in the UK. In time, the means to create a substitute renewable feedstock will be developed and this research is already taking place, but raising the price of gas does not mean it can be developed any faster. There is no way to escape costs in the present, so the government is wrong to claim that it acts as an incentive—there is nothing to incentivise yet.

2

The Present: Britain is Pricing
Itself Out of the Market

When assessing the price at which carbon emissions should be penalised, the government should be looking at the international context in which its policies will reverberate. For example, if every other nation were to set a standard price of £30 per tonne of CO_2 emissions, the UK could also do this without any consequences as all companies worldwide would be paying this price, the cost of which could be passed on to their consumers without affecting their overall competitive advantage. To this extent, the EU-wide climate change tariffs are manageable, forcing all European companies to conform to the same standards—provided this level is not high enough to force emigration from the EU region altogether. Phil Bailey suggested this equality with European rivals meant Lucite has been able to cope with high gas prices in recent times:

> What's actually improved is our competitiveness versus mainland Europe—we've seen less differentiation in gas prices between UK and Europe than were experienced five or so years ago and for us this is the most important thing. Absolutely high energy prices are not an issue if everyone is seeing them, which is now the case, but wasn't in the high costs of 2005. What I am concerned about is more legislation being passed, something you don't see in other regions of the world.

If, however, the UK were to continue to increase the cost of energy and emissions, above levels being paid by competitors, companies located in Britain would see their profits suffer and consequently might emigrate. The

> *The likelihood of this emigration increases as the gap between the costs of UK production and production elsewhere grows.*

likelihood of this emigration increases as the gap between the costs of UK production and production elsewhere grows. Clearly, this is something that should be avoided, but the self-imposed drive to cut emissions at 1990 levels by 34 per cent by 2020, while the rest of Europe looks to reduce them by 20 per cent, is asking for too much in too short a timeframe.

The EU's Emission Trading System

In chemical production, continental Europe is a close rival and direct competitor of the UK. As discussed earlier (p. 3), in theory, the EU ETS should impose similar costs on producers whether they are based in Runcorn or the Ruhr.

Chemical firms will be significantly affected by the EU ETS, so much so that BIS is already concerned about their future. The issue here is twofold:

1. The Directive charges those producing CO_2 emissions a cost proportional to the level of their pollution, with the aim that this will incentivise industries to minimise their carbon output. In the chemicals sector, some firms, like GrowHow, will be directly hit as carbon dioxide is one of the by-products of their industrial processes.

2. Others, such as INEOS Chlor, use electricity as their feedstock and they will be hit indirectly. The cost of the electricity supply will rise as power stations will also have to pay for their emissions. However, as chemical companies cannot simply stop using electricity, the power generating companies can just transfer this extra cost onto these end-users. In order to remain competitive, the chemical manufacturers are not necessarily able to pass their added cost onto the consumer.

The EU ETS charges by the tonne of CO_2 and Stan Higgins has estimated that 'anything approaching £30 per tonne of CO_2 will be prohibitive' to UK chemical production. While current costs are around €15/tCO_2, Deutsche Bank predicts tariffs will be traded at €25/tCO_2 by 2012 and €30-€40/tCO_2 for the third phase of the EU ETS without even taking into consideration the UK's own additional levies.[1]

The crucial issue with the EU ETS is that it imposes costs that competitors outside the EU do not have to bear. Depending on the eventual pricing, this could endanger the entire European chemical industry and, combined with other EU taxes, could push the sector out of the continent to countries where environmental and energy concerns are nil. The impact of the EU ETS can be seen in Figures 5 & 6 (pp. 83, 84), where it is the single largest cost that British chemical companies will face, and it will have an instant effect when Phase III comes into action, increasing costs from 2012-13 by an estimated £1.4 million. In particular, GrowHow faces an extra £3 to £5 million per annum on their bottom line and Deborah Pritchard Jones predicted: 'the industry could become unviable [in the UK] from 2013, it all depends on the EU ETS'.

Not only does the EU ETS restrict the current output of companies, it reduces their potential for growth as well. Phil Bailey argued: 'we are looking to continue to expand the site's capacity and we don't yet actually know and understand if we will be allowed to do that and be given extra allocations to do that. Our view is that we probably won't be.'

The EU ETS is a painful burden, but given Britain cannot back out of it without leaving the EU altogether, the chemical industry must learn to bear it. The government would be wise to refrain from adding further costs on top of this.

Britain is paying the price for the failure of other EU states

Via some EU regulations, Britain is being forced to enact climate change legislation that fails to take into account the fact that the UK has been reducing its GHG emissions far more than most other European countries. Instead of rewarding or even acknowledging this, EU rules aimed at forcing the worst offenders to curb their emissions take a blanket form and compel Britain to do this further as well.

One such unhelpful policy is the EU's Industrial Emissions Directive (IED), which came into force in 2010. This is wide ranging and will affect 52,000 plants across Europe, including chemical producers. It has further cut the existing permitted emission levels of nitrogen oxides, sulphur dioxide and particles allowed from 2016. The IED will force firms to upgrade their plants or install cleaning technology into existing facilities. There will now be further diversion of profits, but this is more towards changing how companies comply with the regulation than actually reducing emissions.

The effect of the Industrial Emissions Directive on power generation

The IED will have a huge impact on Britain's ability to produce electricity. The Directive will come into force from 2016 and power generators must meet the targets it has set or close by 2023.

Countries are being allowed to take advantage of 'national transitional plans', giving generators until June 2020 to comply. If Britain fails to take advantage of this, the new regulations could lead to 25 per cent of British power stations being forced to close, a rise on the shut up from the 15 per cent already expected to close by 2016.

Unless new power stations are built and come on-stream in the near future, the IED will significantly endanger UK security of power supply and will likely cause a price hike and the importation of energy. This will affect everyone, manufacturers and domestic users alike.

The key issue is that many countries have failed to implement the legislation that preceded it, namely, the 2007 Integrated Pollution and Control Directive. Eleven countries are now currently facing infringement actions from the European Commission for failing to meet its requirements, so their commitment to the new IED is doubtful.[2] Fiona Ferguson stated: 'it is questionable how the IED will be any more effectively enforced by those Member States yet to implement the previous legislation properly whilst the UK and a few others lead the way'. Some states, especially in Eastern Europe, are given more flexibility than the UK to meet common targets and extensions have been offered, when they fail to meet them, instead of punitive measures.

The green issue should be framed within a realisation that the problem is less Britain's emission output and more that other countries refuse to take responsibility and curb their emissions. What should be an equal penalty across Europe is therefore not. Countries failing to enforce green regulation are passively aiding their industries in a manner that is unfair to countries like the UK who take the obligations seriously. What is needed is a clampdown on those countries and companies who avoid compliance. Similarly, a continual increase in emission targets is not the way forward as only countries like Britain will take them seriously. Without a new stance of pressuring compliance, overall emissions in Europe will not be decreased and UK industry will suffer unnecessarily.

Gold-plating of EU regulations

Britain has adopted punishing EU green regulations unquestion-ingly, but the real issue is that the government has also gone above and beyond these, exceeding targets other European countries are only just willing to meet. Known as 'gold-plating', this phenomenon has been highly damaging and put British businesses at a disadvantage within Europe. Jeremy Nicholson argued:

> *The Climate Change Act which goes well beyond anything Europe would ever have asked us to do.*

> There are differences in terms of approach to energy and climate even when it comes to working towards common European targets... certainly Britain is going for the gold-plated approach—the classic case is the Climate Change Act which goes well beyond anything Europe would ever have asked us to do, and on renewables where we should never have signed up to the target on this.

The recent Labour government promised far more than it could hope to deliver in terms of renewable power. In accepting the EU Renewable Energy Directive (see p. 2), it committed the country to a burden-sharing agreement which would see the UK obliged to achieve the fastest European renewables growth, while also paying for around a quarter of the total EU's costs. This was signed up to without considering whether the target could actually be met, and in all likelihood, Britain will fail to do so, despite billions of pounds being injected into the scheme. Nicholson summed the situation up: 'there are a whole host of European countries that one cannot imagine would have signed up to that thing in the way we have'.

Going over and above EU regulations can have a real effect on the competitive ability of companies. For example, Lucite has expanded into Eastern Europe, which has no regional producers of MMA and is therefore a ripe market. Phil Bailey argued this meant, 'our disadvantage in shipping to the Eastern Bloc is only relative to producers in France and Germany and transporting it overland from there is not much cheaper'. If the UK imposes extra costs though, this relative equality is lost and other European MMA producers will take control of the market.

Thankfully, Vince Cable, the Secretary of State for Business, has recently announced that Britain will end gold-plating:

> The new principles are a first step towards working with British business and Europe to make sure that we introduce EU rules in a way that will not harm the UK economy. By cutting the red-tape that can reduce competitiveness and making sure that businesses are involved in the process both before, and after through five-yearly reviews, we can get the best deal possible for British companies.[3]

This is a positive sea-change and if Cable is truly looking to redress the balance, then investigating the regulatory impact on the chemicals sector is an optimum place to start.

EU Case study: The move to 30 per cent by 2020

The recent lobbying from Chris Huhne for the EU to raise its 2020 emission reduction targets from 20 per cent to 30 per cent appear likely to undermine Cable's aims. Such a shift would be gold-plating on an epic trans-European scale and would damage the whole region's industrial ability. Chris Huhne has said:

> We would like to be more ambitious at an EU level… we want to move in the EU to a 30 per cent reduction by 2020. The science tells us this is absolutely crucial and we need to ramp up our level of ambition. It is necessary for our sheer economic self-interest precisely because it will send out clearer carbon price signals and allows us to develop more rapidly across all those low-carbon sectors.[4]

The current aim is for the EU ETS to be more damaging than it needs to be by pressing for a tighter cap in addition to the UK taking its own actions to raise the cost of carbon-intensive manufacturing. Furthermore, as has been seen, other EU countries have failed to meet the targets that Britain adheres to, and the government cannot be sure that this would not happen again. Jeremy Nicholson said:

> The industry was not consulted about this… The idea that we will [move to 30 per cent] unilaterally, regardless of whether anyone else in the world bothers to come to the table with anything at all… flagellate ourselves further than we were going to do anyway—I think its reprehensible'.

Europe's main rivals in the chemicals sector are countries such as China that can produce the same product but at a far cheaper cost. This is true throughout all manufacturing, and in chemicals the CIA is concerned with a rise in the Far East's competitive advantage. However, this is perceived by the organisation as temporary with the potential to fall through higher production costs and demands for better wages. Similarly, while the Middle East may be an attractive place to base chemical plants now, due to plentiful fossil fuel supplies,

> *Europe's main rivals in the chemicals sector are countries such as China that can produce the same product but at a far cheaper cost.*

this will dry up in the coming decades. While international competition will even out, Fiona Ferguson felt: 'the area which will have a competitive angle now is regulation and if the EU go on their own to -30 per cent carbon emissions instead of -20 per cent now… that is a problem'. Thus, while China's competitive advantage might not increase, Europe's advantage certainly has the potential to be artificially damaged through government intervention.

Deutsche Bank has estimated: 'If the Commission, as it has recently hinted, raises the target to 30 per cent by 2020, we expect the carbon price to rise to between €30–€35/tonne in 2012 and €48/tonne by 2020.'[5] The faster Europe and the UK's production costs rise, the more they will outweigh the obstacles of time, cost and effort associated with transporting chemicals internationally and indeed the barriers to emigration itself.

Unilateral policies

Even if the whole EU agreed on reducing emissions by 30 per cent by 2020, Britain would still be penalising industry more via its commitment to a 34 per cent emission decrease by 2020 under the Climate Change Act. This unilateral ambition has given rise to levies unique to Britain such as the Renewables Obligation that will drive up chemical firms' costs, regardless of the situation in any other country. Chris Huhne's claim that Britain is better off being 'ahead of the pack' on climate change is fundamentally untrue, there is no evidence that suggests there is a benefit in maintaining higher production costs than competitors.

It is never a good idea to raise the costs of production in one country relative to another, but when the rivalry between countries is as intensive as it is between Britain and places like Holland, the outcome is even worse. According to Stan Higgins, NEPIC's strongest competition for investment is from Rotterdam and Antwerp, both

> *The UK cannot expect any investment from foreign investors, even low-carbon ones, if it prices itself above competitors who would never shackle their industries in this manner.*

also successful chemical centres: 'if you have an investor looking at Teesside, it's a hell of a fight to persuade them not to put it in either of the other two'. The UK cannot expect any investment from foreign investors, even low-carbon ones, if it prices itself above competitors who would never shackle their industries in this manner. Defenders of this long standing approach to tackling climate change argue that existing capital investments will not be abandoned even if costs rise, but this is untrue. Existing British chemical firms will fold or emigrate to wherever production is cheapest while multinational firms will channel their funds to other plants: these actions have always been the norm.

> ## Germany's take on funding renewables
>
> Even in countries that are reducing their emissions to a similar extent compared to Britain, the firms involved are not having to foot the entire bill. In Germany, chemical firms and wider energy intensive sectors are given significant concessions when paying compulsory domestic renewable levies, despite Germany having invested more in this.
>
> As in Britain, the German chemical industry is a key exporter and has a promising future if nurtured. Its overall importance has meant contributions for the majority of the renewable costs are offset to other, less critical sectors. The German exemptions are symptomatic of a country that values its manufacturing and understands its national economic importance in a way that Britain does not.

British cost-raising initiatives make non-British clusters look far more attractive, and firms there already receive far greater support as it is, with infrastructure within the publicly-owned ports being paid for entirely from the public purse. In contrast, the Teesport and other export centres can only hope for a maximum of 20 per cent funding from the British government. Combined with rising energy and carbon costs, there is now an atmosphere of pessimism amongst potential investors when faced with the situation in the North East. Higgins explained:

> I met the new president of the Indian Chemical Council and he's building a new factory in Europe, so I suggested visiting the North East of England. He said he's been told that chemical industry is migrating from Britain into Europe and wasn't this the case? These are the

messages he's getting… we have to be out there fighting the position and showing that's not necessarily the case—but it might be too late.

This should be a cause for concern, especially as India, Brazil and other countries have begun to saturate their domestic chemical markets and are looking to invest outwards: Britain cannot appear to be a backwater.

Unilateral policy study: the Carbon Price Floor

The Carbon Price Floor (CPF) was introduced in the eponymous report of December 2010 and was given the go-ahead in the March 2011 Budget.[6] It will be implemented as a reform of the Climate Change Levy. The key points of the CPF:

- This is the first policy of its kind worldwide.

- It will artificially establish a minimum price on emission permits of £30/tCO_2 by 2020.

- The CPF will come into force in 2013, at the same time as the EU ETS Phase III. This means that if the European carbon market prices a tonne of CO_2 below the CPF, UK companies will pay more than their European rivals. This mechanism is shown in Figure 7 (p. 85).

- The CCL will charge a new 'carbon price support rate' tax on fossil fuels like coal as well as gas and liquid petroleum gas (LPG). Oil will also be taxable but with a rate of its own. These were previously exempt from the CCL.

The CPF had two main purposes:

1. It is designed to tax fossil fuels according to their carbon content with the hope that this will 'encourage greater investment in low-carbon electricity generation' via the CPF.[7]

2. The CPF is a unilateral levy on top of the EU-wide EU ETS because: 'there is uncertainty about how carbon prices will evolve and a question about whether the carbon price delivered through the EU ETS is strong and stable enough to drive the decarbonisation required'.[8]

For anyone involved in the chemical industry, it is clear such a unilateral tax is unwise. Not only is no other country in the world doing this, but it also undermines the existing rough equality of costs with Europe. Indeed, by going over and above the EU ETS, Britain is engaging in the worst gold-plating to date.

The government has estimated the additional cost of the CPF to energy-intensive industries to be an increase of between two per cent and six per cent on electricity bills.[9] This may not seem large on paper, but using the data from Figure 6 (p. 84), an addition of that size in 2013 would cost an average company between £60,000 and £180,000 and this would be rising over time. The CPF will drive the cost to the £30 cut-off that Higgins estimated to be lethal to some companies (see p. 32) and by 2030, the price is planned to rise to £70/tCO$_2$. This pushes the cost too high too soon, before new technological means of efficiency can be designed and implemented. The CPF is an embodiment of all the unilateral errors being made by the government in the name of rapid carbon reduction and is simply unworkable. The EU ETS, if implemented across Europe equally, is a much fairer mechanism and imposes bearable, gentler costs.

DECC's lack of support

The pursuit of unilateral climate-change policies and a lack of tough negotiating at an EU-level suggest the Department for Energy and Climate has little concern for the UK. Its strong influence over the government has meant that help for manufacturing will only be delivered via general minor measures—such as the incoming reduction in corporation tax as outlined in the *Growth Review*.

> *The pursuit of unilateral climate-change policies and a lack of tough negotiating at an EU-level suggest the Department for Energy and Climate has little concern for the UK.*

Any relief for energy-intensive sectors in relation to green issues will be seen by DECC as 'comprise of principles' that undermines their role. Deborah Pritchard Jones said:

> [DECC] perceive taking a climate change leadership role as a vote winner... It isn't that DECC don't want to fight our corner—they will

and do fight our corner, but they have no incentive to do this at the cost of compromising the overarching principles required to be 'the greenest government ever'.

The impression we've had from DECC is that they are delighted that the more industry is removed from the UK, the lower our emissions are.

Jeremy Nicholson stated the problem is actually worse: 'the impression we've had from DECC is that they are delighted that the more industry is removed from the UK, the lower our emissions are. They literally are not concerned about the international dimensions.'

On the other hand, the Department of Business, Innovation and Skills has been far more aware of the importance of the chemicals sector and has therefore been trying to fight the industry's corner, as seen in the reversal of the Renewable Heat Incentive. DECC had pushed for the RHI despite the fact that it was a very inefficient way to reduce industrial pollution. DECC even admitted: 'the RHI as a whole fails to pass the cost effectiveness test'.[10] It had been rushed through Parliament prior to the 2010 General Election but since then was successfully scrapped with pressure from BIS, when its potentially devastating nature was realised. The changes have meant that there will still be a level of renewable heat sources available in the future, which is itself a highly desirable outcome, but without jeopardising energy-intensive firms—the optimum result.

These situations can emerge because, unlike BIS, DECC doesn't have to take the actual practical effect of regulations into account to the same degree, which is a convenient way for the Department to 'bury its head in the sand' and willingly propose and accept impractical targets. The solution is for joined-up government, where all the Departments cooperate to accurately assess the state of the industry. BIS, DECC and the Treasury should work together to balance taxes against economic contributions as well as energy and emissions efficiency and pin these to the relative levels of competitors.

3

The Future: How the Low-carbon Economy is being Jeopardised

At one time, the chemicals sector was a heavy generator of emissions including carbon dioxide, nitrous oxide and other harmful gases. However, while chemical production has cleaned up and improved, its image has not. There is still the assumption that manufacturing chemicals is a dirty business, while the large consumption of energy required by the industry has meant it appears to be responsible for copious net carbon emissions. Both these statements are untrue and the facts reveal a very different picture. The chemical industry is part of the solution to climate change, not part of the problem, and if nothing is done to recognise the industry's contribution, its loss will be sorely felt.

When the Coalition was formed in May 2010, David Cameron promised Britain 'the greenest government ever', but from the actions taken so far, this appears false.[1] Instead of nurturing the chemicals sector's ability to equip Britain with the resources vital to the LCE, the focus is on making

> *The fight against GHG emissions is not a sprint but a marathon, and the Government should avoid trying to win political green points at the expense of long-term improvements.*

quick carbon cuts in the lifetime of this parliament that will satisfy the targets set for 2020. These rapid reductions, which rely on energy-intensive sectors such as chemicals simply disappearing from the UK and the GHG balance sheet, will make the long-term target of an 80 per cent reduction by 2050 and development beyond this much harder to meet. The fight against GHG emissions is not a sprint but a marathon, and the government should avoid trying to win political green points at the expense of long-term improvements.

Cutting its own emissions

The chemical industry has gone a long way towards minimising the pollution caused by its production processes and in 2007 the industry spent £655 million on 'environmental expenditure', just over a quarter of the total amount spent by all British manufacturers.[2] This includes all aspects of combating climate change, from preventing pollution to educational programmes. Waters Wye found that 'by the end of this year [2010], UK emissions of N_2O from nitric acid production will become the lowest in Europe'.[3] As a whole, the CIA organises a Responsible Care programme and subscribing firms are obliged to improve their impact on the environment year-on-year. The chemical industry is not resting on its laurels.

GrowHow's unavoidable CO_2 emissions

Ammonia production creates CO_2 as an inevitable by-product. According to Deborah Pritchard Jones: 'the overall carbon footprint of our products is very low, but there is less we can do for our ammonia plants and we've done what we can'.

GrowHow's highly advanced plant ensures the CO_2 is as clean as it can be. This waste is then commercially used in other CO_2-dependent processes such as carbonating drinks. In total, GrowHow provides three quarters of the UK's CO_2 supply. Any excess CO_2 is supplied to a neighbouring commercial greenhouse which houses 300,000 tomato plants producing their fruit throughout the year, thereby avoiding the carbon footprint of importing tomatoes in the winter months.

Despite producing vast quantities of CO_2, GrowHow has turned this into an advantage that benefits all.

There are some unavoidable by-products of chemical processes, though, that are too difficult to re-use. Fiona Ferguson said: 'there are occasions where the most cost-effective and environmentally sensible thing to do is to landfill, so we need to make sure things like that are recognised'. Despite the appearance, landfilling is often cheaper in terms of minimising pollution when the alternative method of elimination requires extremely high quantities of energy. While this won't be the case forever, as the example of PYReco shows (see p. 50), the government needs to be aware that image isn't everything and green policies should not be pursued to the extent that they undermine actual emissions reduction. Instead, there should be a greater balance and understanding in policies of the complex and subtle relationships between energy use, raw material recovery/conservation and space requirements.

Efficiency-inhibiting regulations

The existing issue of over-regulation has had the curious effect of actually hampering attempts by the chemical industry to improve its energy consumption and reduce its reliance on fossil fuels. Firms such as INEOS Chlor have tried to diversify their energy sources and move into funding their own independent renewable schemes. For example, INEOS has been constructing an 'energy from waste' plant at its Runcorn site at a cost of £400 million to produce 20 per cent of its energy requirements. However, despite the government's commitment to increasing the use of such schemes, companies are having trouble setting them up due to the lingering perceptions of waste incinerators as dirty and a health risk, and it is taking time and effort to combat these assumptions.[4] In addition, a situation has emerged in some areas where local waste is already being taken to an incinerator in a different location so a new one would have to ship in waste rather than maximise its carbon efficiency by being allowed to burn local refuse. The trials and tribulations experienced by INEOS sends a negative message to other firms looking into similar strategies.

The hostility to chemical recycling has also increased. For example, chemical companies used to burn their own waste by-products to produce heat, thus reducing their consumption of oil. This has now been stopped by EU regulations on the basis of the pollution it creates, despite the fact that modern advances in recycling methods mean that emissions are heavily reduced and energy is conserved in the process.

Similarly, the British government appears to have taken a dim view of by-product recycling, on the basis that it doesn't fit into their classifications of what constitutes recycling under the EU's Waste Incineration Directive (WID). NEPIC has been struggling with this and Stan Higgins explained:

> The WID regulation says if you recycle something within a process it's a waste. No it isn't! It's used again in the process. The civil servants say, 'oh well it was a waste to start with', but no, it's a by-product which we re-use. We end up with a really complicated system of regulation and overregulation of what happens within factories. There is an insidious implementation of policies—we apply them to the letter but have no room for interpretation.

The inflexibility of current regulations is symptomatic of a bureaucracy, both at UK and EU levels, that lacks the necessary specialist knowledge to understand the consequences of what might otherwise seem sound policy. Forcing companies to conform to such rules is unwise and fails to reflect the technical nature of chemical product. To improve the regulatory structure, firms' concerns and expertise should be taken into greater consideration.

The chemical industry is the foundation of the low-carbon economy

On the subject of the chemical industry, Chris Huhne said, 'recovery doesn't come from old industries bouncing back… the low-carbon industries will be an important part of our growth story over the next ten years'.[5] Huhne's comment suggests that a successful sector that has survived over a century is no longer valued, by virtue of its age. It also implies the chemical industry is in stasis, when it is not: the industry has risen to the challenge of combating climate change and is manufacturing the products necessary to combat it. It *is* a low-carbon industry.

Chemicals are vital—from contributing to carbon-efficient products to energy-saving catalysts. Basic chemicals often provide the raw materials for these goods: chlorine, for example, is a key component used in manufacturing insulating material. Similarly, speciality chemicals are being developed and used in specific products such as synthetic rubbers in fuel-saving tyres. The emission-reducing role that all chemicals are involved in will only grow as demand for them increases.

Independent research by McKinsey carried out for the CIA found that, on average, for every tonne of emissions produced in chemical production, two tonnes are saved down the line via the products, in other words, an emissions saving ratio of 2:1.[6] This can rise to an astounding extent and for manufactured insulating materials, 233 times the amount of CO_2 emitted in production is saved over its life cycle.[7] This means that one year's production of this insulation enables 2.4 billion tonnes of CO_2 to be saved, the equivalent of four times the total GHG emissions of the UK.[8] While other non-chemical based insulating materials do exist, they are not as efficient or inexpensive to manufacture.

> **Some examples of emissions savings ratios**
>
> 233:1 Insulation
>
> 123:1 Wind turbine blade materials
>
> 71:1 Lightweight aeroplane components
>
> 51:1 Fuel-saving tyres
>
> 9:1 Low temperature detergents
>
> 2.7:1 PVC windows
>
> 2.6:1 Synthetic textiles
>
> 2.3:1 Domestic polymer piping
>
> 2.2:1 Use of enzymes to increase the life of bread
>
> 2:1 Average saving across the industry
>
> 1.8:1 Polymers replacing traditional packaging
>
> (Source: Chemical Industries Association, The Chemical Industry: delivering a low-carbon future 24 hours a day)

If Chris Huhne and the government really want Britain simultaneously to develop its advanced manufacturing *and* become a LCE, then they must recognise that the chemicals sector is integral to this and qualifies for both descriptions through the products and innovations it supplies. The government has made much of so-called 'high-tech' manufacturing, and the *Growth Review* makes special mention of sectors such as 'aerospace, defence... micro-electronics'. All these and more are reliant on the yields of the chemical industry for their success and future growth.[9] Stan Higgins said: 'if we want to become a high-tech haven in a low-carbon future, there will be huge factories beavering away making special materials and we want those things to be made here as well as consumer products'. The sector's contribution has only just begun, and it would be very short-sighted to suggest that it should be judged on the basis of its back record rather than its new future.

> *If Chris Huhne and the government really want Britain simultaneously to develop its advanced manu-facturing and become a LCE, then they must recognise that the chemicals sector is integral to this.*

The definition of 'green' companies is flawed

Short-term carbon-reducing plans appear to be clouding awareness of the fact that the chemical industry is environmentally beneficial and should not be forced out of the country. Jeremy Nicholson argued:

> With a sudden rush of blood to the head they [politicians] decide that our energy is going to come from offshore wind turbines without working out where the materials that are going to be used in their production will come from... without which you can't build them. The disconnect there is so large it would be laughable were it not unfortunately the norm.

> *The definition of what constitutes 'low-carbon' as politicians understand it is flawed, and is far more complex than has previously been assumed.*

The ethos of climate-change policies is all about reducing emissions as fast as possible and, as part of this rushed effort, the measures used by government to gauge whether an industry is 'green' or not fail to paint an accurate picture of the industry's real carbon footprint. Examining only the levels of energy feeding into chemical plants, as the majority of carbon regulations do, is not a realistic indication of how green a company is.

Instead, the entire process and product must be taken into account to gain a properly holistic indication. Such an approach reveals a very different picture as the following two examples demonstrate:

1. PVC is used in the most efficient energy-saving window frames and has an emissions saving ratio of 2.7:1. In Britain, it is solely at the energy-intensive INEOS ChlorVinyls plant in Runcorn, Cheshire.[10] Without the chemical plant, either the PVC or the frames would have to be imported, raising costs and transport emissions.

2. A chemical plant in the NEPIC cluster produces transition lenses for glasses, using alternative materials with higher emissions than their rivals. However, while their rivals' products have a life expectancy of three to four years, this company's lenses continue to work way beyond this and the glasses have a longer lifecycle. Hence, while the initial emissions from the chemical might be greater, their extended use compared to alternative materials justifies this.

The definition of what constitutes 'low-carbon' as politicians understand it is flawed, and is far more complex than has previously been assumed.

The cost of 'green living' will rise

The current energy and climate-change plans will create a perverse situation where many companies developing low-carbon innovations will be driven out of business before they can market their products. The only way for companies to survive higher costs will be to pass these on to their customers, and consumer product prices will consequently rise. This will be the case for many goods, from lipsticks to fabric softeners, but the government should be most worried about the rising cost that would occur for energy- and emission–saving products. If the industries were to emigrate, chemicals would have to be imported. The low-carbon industries Chris Huhne claims to have identified rely on the chemicals sector and their existence is not mutually exclusive as he assumes. To eliminate the so-called 'old industry' would smother the LCE at birth and strike at the heart of emerging sectors.

Given that one of the main challenges of promoting a 'green society' is the higher cost of low-carbon living for the consumer when compared to their normal lifestyle, the government should aim to keep these costs to a minimum. Rather than having to provide subsidies to homes to do this, the same benefits can be derived by reducing energy levies so that the producing companies can provide their goods at the lowest cost.

Company Case Study: PYReco and tyre recycling

The contribution of the chemicals sector to the fight against climate change is not always acknowledged, something that is a major problem. There appears to be a reluctance to modify regulation to adapt to the innovations of the chemicals sector, and instead it appears that the firms themselves are expected to adapt. This was demoralising to PYReco who 'very nearly did emigrate' according to Higgins and in the end it decided to stay due to the significant problem with tyre waste the UK has and the potential for a future market.

This hardly paints a picture of a dynamically green government, but more perverse was the response from the quango Waste and Resources Action Programme (WRAP). WRAP's self-proclaimed aims are 'a world without waste, where resources are used sustainably' and 'to deliver a lighter carbon footprint for the UK'.[11] Despite PYReco's innovation fitting perfectly with this brief, Higgins recounted:

> Saying to this man at WRAP that Britain has a problem with tyres, he replied: 'Don't say we have a problem, we have not got a problem with tyres—we can burn them in cement kilns.' That's great—we have all that carbon captured in a wheel and we're just going to stick it back in the air again. That's not what we want to do, is it?

Background to PYReco

PYReco is a start-up company in the NEPIC cluster that has developed the means to adapt pyrolysis to break down rubber tyres into their constituent materials. Usual pyrolysis involves the thermal breakdown of organic materials at very high temperatures in the absence of oxygen. This new process requires only a moderate amount of heat.

There is no waste from PYReco's process. From the 60,000 tonnes it estimates it can process annually in its initial phase, 21,373 tonnes of carbon black and 8,107 tonnes of steel will be reclaimed. Per day, 66 tonnes of gas and 51 tonnes oil will also be produced, to generate around 232.32 MWh of power.

If all the tyres in Europe were treated by PYReco, the consumption of six million barrels of oil would be saved and 700,000 tonnes of CO_2 emissions would be avoided per year. If all the discarded tyres in Britain were treated according to the process it has developed, one to two per cent of the entire UK's carbon footprint would be saved. The Carbon Trust produced a report into the company and found:

> If the use of PYReco pyrolysis was extrapolated to recover all the tyres from the UK market... this would require about 8 similar pyrolysis plants... giving a total net lifecycle benefit of 666,451 tonnes CO_2e per annum. There may also be additional avoided GHG emissions from diverting the tyre waste from other disposal routes.

Clearly, the potential benefits of PYReco are huge and have great growth potential given that old tyres abound worldwide. Within the UK, the need for eight more plants would employ many and further entrench the UK's already established relationship between the chemical industry and LCE. In theory, this is one of the developments the Government should be delighted to hear about. Despite this, Stan Higgins claimed that PYReco had huge difficulties in explaining to Government representatives that this was worthwhile:

> They couldn't get their heads round it. I was in the meeting with them, and they said, 'Well hold on, what is this? It's not re-use, because you're not putting the tyre on a different car. It's not recycling, because you don't get everything back—we don't know what to do!' In the end, they categorised it between the two and it took 18 months to get to that position.

WRAP's judgement suggests a conservative nature, where recycling and other green ideas are framed within a context of what is possible in the here-and-now, rather than looking to the innovations of the future. Britain should not be content to burn tyres *ad infinitum* simply because this fits the description of 'waste to energy'.

The lack of enthusiasm that the government has so far shown towards such possible revolutions does a great disservice to the industry. It should not be NEPIC's purpose to have to fight against this lack of understanding. Further innovations could be encouraged through a swift recognition of their worth and an eagerness to adopt them, thus seeding the real LCE.

Declining investment

The contribution of the chemical industry to combating climate change will increase in the future, but within a long-term timeframe as innovations and catalysts are developed. The McKinsey study suggests that if a more sympathetic governmental policy framework were put into action, where industry is not priced out of existence, by 2030 the emissions saving ratio would double to 4:1, outweighing any green 'benefits' derived from the forced emigration of the sector.

As stated earlier, the industry's own carbon footprint is shrinking, but it has reached a point where further reductions rely on big investments—something that will not be forthcoming if the future of the industry does not appear certain. Fiona Ferguson stated:

> They've done all the obvious stuff about changing pumps, insulating things getting power from the residual heat... that's been done since 1990 so the next big change is in catalyst technology and building new plants... there's only so much you can do with an old one.

The building of these new plants is obviously investment intensive, which explains why few have been built in Britain, as they would commit firms to the UK despite the rising costs of production here. Deborah Pritchard Jones suggested that these costs had now hit the level where long-term emigration was likely. She said:

> There is no point investing in a new UK plant and there won't be any new ammonium plants in the UK or Europe now. If you're going to

build one, it will be in Saudi or Egypt where you can get... gas price deals [that] are all long term and are either fixed or based on a known index that manages energy price exposure risk.

GrowHow is fighting for business in a highly competitive marketplace where its main competitors are globally based, setting the odds against the British firm. The understandable unwillingness to invest further in GrowHow's ageing plant means that it is increasingly vulnerable to even small shifts in production costs which cannot be passed on to the end-user.

The medium-term mixed economy

The low-carbon economy will not spring into mainstream existence overnight. No matter how punitive the hidden costs and add-on levies, companies cannot switch their production or consumption as rapidly as the government hopes its 'incentives' will ensure. Similarly, not all Britons will buy an electric or alternative fuel car as their next automobile—the uptake will be slow to begin with, even if they eventually outnumber conventional cars in the future. For the next few decades at least, Britain will have a mixed carbon usage economy, where fossil fuels are used, albeit decreasingly, alongside newer technologies and it must be recognised that the chemicals sector will maintain production according to demand and will rely on revenues from petrochemicals for a good while longer.

The government has been looking too far into the future and it has failed to consider properly how Britain will remain economically viable in the meantime before fledgling low-carbon industries develop. Chris Huhne has complained:

> The institutional structure of society as it is overemphasises those with vested interest in the old economic structure and underemphasises the jobs and the companies that are still a glint in the eye... [we have] a level of risk aversion and a responsiveness to vested interest that is not perhaps rational.

The problem with this idea is that it requires a prioritisation of embryonic industries over highly profitable existing ones. For the country as a whole, it is unrealistic to expect the national economy to survive a period without either new or existing industries. Moreover, the new sectors will essentially rely on most of the skills that the older ones have required, so maintaining and entrenching these older industries is vital to success and rejuvenation. The LCE is not a phoenix that will rise from the ashes of the chemicals sector.

> *The low-carbon economy is not a phoenix that will rise from the ashes of the chemicals sector.*

Huhne is mistaken on the origin of the above 'risk aversion' as well. It belongs to multinational companies, not the UK. His expectation that 'moving to 30 per cent will provide greater certainty and predictability for investors,' is only true insofar as it confirms to foreign investors that Britain is hostile to industry.[12] Chemical companies looking to invest in the UK will reject it on the basis that 'leading the pack' on climate change is too risky for their business.

Johnson Matthey

Johnson Matthey is a chemical company developing ideal low-carbon technology in the form of new, specialised catalysts and fuel cells that will work on hydrogen-based equipment.

While this research is still progressing, uptake of the new catalysts for the next few years will be slow. The firm is thus still reliant on producing catalysts for fossil fuel engine cars and petrochemical industries.

During this phase, it will still be vulnerable to energy costs, as will its customers. If the large market for the catalysts used by the oil industry is not sustained, Johnson Matthey's low-carbon catalyst development could be negatively impacted.

It will take time for the adjustment to take effect. While some chemical products and technologies are easily transferable to new low-carbon markets, most will need to be developed from scratch. For much of the foreseeable future, these markets (such as for hydrogen fuel cells) will grow parallel to fossil fuel-based ones rather than immediately supersede them. The UK economy and its businesses need to be given the time to adapt to these changes. Lucite, for example, is doing research into using a bio-based feedstock rather than natural gas. Once this comes to fruition, this plant could easily be built in Britain, if the conditions were right. Phil Bailey said:

> I'm sure it will come, be it 15 or 20 years, and when it does, I want the existing plant still to be here so that we will already have a site for it. We have to hang around with existing technology long enough while inexorably driving down the cost base to keep ourselves as competitive as possible.

The government must be more realistic and recognise that the LCE is a long-term goal which needs similarly paced policies in place to support it.

Increasing carbon leakage

Chris Huhne has repeatedly argued in favour of implementing greater carbon tariffs and energy taxes than any other country. Contrary to his suggestions that the UK would benefit from this: there are no tangible advantages to pricing ourselves out of the market. In addition to the domestic problems and loss of revenue already discussed, the emigration of industries would lead to carbon leakage. While this term is routinely applied to carbon emissions, it must be remembered that the chemical industry has the potential to release a diverse range of additional damaging by-products.

In a global context, it is clear companies would move from the UK and its high levels of emission regulation to countries where energy is cheap and pollution monitoring minimal—a scenario likely to result in net global emissions rising. While Britain's own national emissions would fall, emigrant companies with no need to lower their GHG output would maintain lower production costs through cheaper, more polluting processes. For example, in some extra-EU countries energy costs are decided by agreement between the firm and the respective nation's government and this is frequently set for a long duration and at a price kept below the market rate. This gives companies far less of an incentive to economise on energy usage. Phil Bailey said: 'carbon leakage is a massive issue. If we don't make

MMA here, it will get made in China or the Middle East where it probably won't be with the same emission requirements.'

China, India and Brazil are building some of the most energy-efficient plants possible, taking advantage of the technologies being developed in countries like the UK such as Johnson Matthey's new catalyst, APICO, which delivers shorter start-up times, longer catalyst life and fewer by-products. The CIA estimates that 'a considerable amount' of Johnson Matthey's customers for this innovation are from these countries compared with the UK. However, these plants are being powered by dirty coal and other polluting fuels, so while energy costs are kept at a minimum for the firms involved, the benefits to the global climate are negated. In addition, these companies can produce their products at a lower cost than the UK, and gain a competitive advantage in the process.

The current policy framework implies carbon leakage does not matter provided Britain meets its targets. This is effectively extreme 'nimbyism'—emissions are acceptable provided they are not on the UK's balance sheet. Clearly, a more sensible and realistic approach is needed. The UK should be contributing to a globally concerted effort to reduce emissions, and needs to ensure that it does not offload these onto other countries. A balance must be struck between encouraging firms to reduce their emissions but also ensuring they remain in the UK where these can be regulated properly. Indeed, while Britain engages in mass handwringing on account of the pollution it produces, a certain level of perspective is needed. Given Britain is only responsible for two per cent of global GHGs, it would do more good to foster the chemical industry and its innovations so the sector can further the worldwide environmental fight.

4

The Wider Picture:
The Downstream Effect

The chemical industry is crucial to the UK, not just because of its direct production and exports, but as a result of the secondary industries it also supports. The Royal Society of Chemistry identified 15 downstream sectors, 'in which chemistry research is a necessary (but not the only) condition for their operation'.[1] These support 5.1 million jobs and directly contributed £222 billion to the UK's GDP in 2007.[2] Chlorine, for example, is manufactured by INEOS Chlor and used in the manufacture of plastics like PVC, solvents, agrochemicals and pharmaceuticals. Additionally, chlorine is required for a diverse range of consumer goods like bleach, computer hardware, silicon chips and cars. The by-products of the chemical production processes also have uses: caustic soda, created in the manufacture of chlorine, has a similarly long list of applications. In addition, other industries have developed to cater to the needs of chemical users, for instance, building delicate equipment that can ensure delivery of a substance to parts per trillion. Jeremy Nicholson said this all created a key competitive advantage:

> What has always been a characteristic of the industry has been that one person's waste is another person's feedstock. It leads to the co-location of sites where one thing feeds directly into another whether they are commonly owned or not. This has also meant there are bright and abled people located within certain areas... this isn't unique but it is a prerequisite for success.

The geographical concentration of chemical firms has been a source of strength for the industry, but is also its Achilles Heel. The companies lean on each other to the extent that if one goes out of business, the others are also weakened and can fall, dragging down entire supply chains. The CIA has estimated that an additional 400,000 workers in the UK directly depend on primary chemical production remaining in the UK. A study of this effect found that in specialised chemicals and pharmaceuticals, four jobs are at risk for every directly related worker, and for more general chemicals, this rises to ten indirect jobs reliant on their continued production.[3]

Their unseen contribution

The threat to the direct chemical industry is serious enough, but these secondary sectors range across many different divisions that are not taken into account by the official statistics relating to the chemical industry. The Office for National Statistics requires all companies to submit an SIC (Standard Industrial Classification) code by which they define which sector they belong to. Stan Higgins elaborated:

> ONS numbers don't work in our industry... most of our companies align themselves with their markets not their industry so my members put themselves to 46 SIC codes when there should only be six. ONS says there's 12,000 working [in the NEPIC area] and they finally admitted there were 35,000 and they said to me 'we've always wondered why, when we do the national census, we could only see 12,000 people working in chemicals but 35,000 people said they did!'

This means that the UK appears to have far less of a chemical industry than it really does. In addition, many chemical companies are owned by foreign firms which only have a London registered office. This has meant there are apparently 200 chemical firms working out of the City of London, while NEPIC has only 105 in the North East![4] As a result, politicians are unaware that the acknowledged chemicals sector is just the tip of the iceberg.

Currently, the government assumes that secondary industries will not leave the UK, even if primary chemical firms do. For example, Chris Huhne has argued that: 'quite of few of the high energy users have forms of natural protection like high transport costs so the impact is rather less than you might expect'.[5] However, if the producers of feedstock chemicals leave, then companies will have little choice but to import it, having to overcome this same high transport costs. If this continues to happen, there will come a point where Britain loses its critical mass as companies relocate to avoid these overheads. Jeremy Nicholson suggested:

> The idea that downstream industries are likely to remain here indefinitely if primary production goes might have a theoretical case, but I'd say just look at the empirical evidence: downstream manufacturing thrives on co-location with primary industry and why would you expect that to cease in future?

There is also an additional risk that downstream industries could quit the UK independently of other variables: commodity chemicals can increasingly be manufactured elsewhere at lower prices, tempting secondary industries abroad. Phil Bailey saw this as an issue Lucite could eventually face: 'downstream companies are fundamental and they are our customer base. Unless you've got the consumers in the region where you manufacture, it takes away one of the big reasons why you want to be in that region'.

Company case study: Dow's ethylene oxide plant

Background to Dow

The Dow plant was the sole ethylene oxide manufacturer in the UK. It was located in Wilton in the NEPIC cluster. Its closure was announced in July 2009, with the final shut-down complete by January 2010. Fifty-five jobs were directly lost at the plant.

The closure was caused by a glut of ethylene glycol on the market, due to two plants producing this coming on-stream in the Middle East. Half of Dow's ethylene oxide was converted into ethylene glycol, but the new foreign plants were able to produce their product at a lower cost that Dow couldn't match, making its entire operation unprofitable.

Real life examples clearly show just how fragile downstream companies are. The decline of Dow is one such instance and Fiona Ferguson explained:

> It's an illustration of how chemical companies all are interdependent. The problem was that the Wilton site used to be an integrated ICI site

and the product flows between individual plants used to be balanced, with the ICI ethylene cracker as the top of the pyramid. Gradually since then, the customer base has declined and declined as it was cheaper for companies to do it abroad. Loss of the ethylene oxide plant took away a demand for ethylene, and led to closure of other plants downstream as well.

While just 55 jobs were lost at the Dow plant, the repercussions were wider reaching within the North East Teesside cluster. The nearby Croda International chemical plant, which was reliant on the supply of ethylene oxide, was then forced to close as well with a loss of a further 125 jobs. In August 2009, Artenius, another local chemical company, collapsed as well with 240 made redundant. While Artenius reopened with 180 jobs saved, it now has to rely on importing its raw materials. Overall, it was estimated that 2,500 jobs were at risk throughout the North East Teesside cluster.[6] NEPIC has taken the loss of Dow in its stride and has claimed that the 'domino' effect of industrial collapse was not as likely as has been made out. Stan Higgins said: 'It would need a huge number of closures and it hasn't happened—it was the two companies Dow and Croda... a lot of the gap has been refilled, although not completely.'

Nonetheless, there is still a need to take the Dow closure and potential for a 'domino' effect seriously as a wake-up call. Phil Bailey said: 'I don't think it's a done deal that it will all close, but it requires us to do some things to prevent this from happening'. The collapse of Dow was not due to funding but the lack of a wide customer supply base. Without this, the long-term future of chemical companies is untenable. The simple solution is not to force the alienation of customers by making production costs rise.

The lack of transport flexibility

The chained effect of industry collapse partially results from the difficulty in importing raw chemicals and the complex logistics of transporting them. The geographic location of the UK is a double-edged sword—exported chemicals can be easily shipped abroad and the UK is perfectly situated to take advantage of many international markets by bypassing expensive continental land. However, it is a very difficult and expensive process to import raw chemicals into the UK due to their material state and often toxic nature. Some are even banned from being transported in the Channel Tunnel, so slow progress by sea is the only option. If the need arose, this might be acceptable for mass produced chemicals where economies of scale make it worthwhile, such as for ammonia, but others like hydrogen cyanide would be very difficult to transport for unsurprising reasons.

Some industrial users, if large enough and able to sacrifice competitive advantage, are able to support the increased costs of importing chemicals and the demand for soap and other products means ethylene oxide is now imported in bulk. However, this outcome is debilitating for everyone. There are environmental costs to consider, as the transportation of chemicals will lead to greater emissions. In addition, the balance of trade incurs a penalty from increased imports. Hence while the scenario is a do-able one, it is not a desirable outcome.

However, the majority of chemical and downstream firms are made up of SMEs whose capacity to absorb the costs of importing are reduced. As secondary users, many would face bankruptcy or relocation to wherever the primary manufacturers settle. This is particularly the case with specialist or hazardous chemicals which cannot be transported by road or rail easily—it has already been seen in the closure of Dow's ethylene oxide plant and the movement of consumer firms to situate near new international plants.

The government must not under-estimate the number of stakeholders relying on the chemicals sector and the disproportionate effect its loss would have. This is a medium to long-term problem that will only get worse if the government prices the UK out of the market. GrowHow and INEOS Chlor have remained in the UK despite rising costs because they respectively produce practically all the British ammonia and

> *The government must recognise that the adherence to its current policies means that the emigration of chemical firms is not a case of 'if' but 'when'.*

chlorine, so demand from other firms has so far been sustained. The government should not make the mistake of assuming they will remain in the UK regardless of production costs: present commitment to the UK doesn't discount a future relocation if profit margins fall further. The government must recognise that the adherence to its current policies means that the emigration of chemical firms is not a case of 'if' but 'when'.

5

A Level Playing Field?

While energy costs and green regulations, at both an EU and national level, are the main concerns for the chemical industry, there are other important issues that add to the existing negative business environment. The key issue is that incentives for companies to develop or invest in the UK are waning, which is especially concerning given that an increasing number of chemical firms are now foreign-owned. This comes at a time when most other countries are eager to secure chemical investments and are not afraid actively to entice these either.

To call these problems 'secondary worries' when comparing them to energy and green costs would do them an injustice: they are as important but are less dramatic in their impact and less simple to solve. Higher costs might price the chemical industry out of the UK, but without these additional concerns being taken into consideration, the sector could just stagnate. Unlike the energy taxes and levies, their solutions rely on the government doing something positive rather than remaining passive.

Other countries provide incentives

Britain is an attractive place to set up a business. It is geographically well placed to take advantage of many markets, and offers a highly skilled workforce. Innovation is important to the chemicals sector, and increasingly so as the pressure to find alternative and efficient power sources mounts. Many chemical firms have traditionally centred their R&D in the UK to take advantage of the high quality of British graduates and higher education facilities. However, as the recent loss of Pfizer from the UK shows, this British competitive advantage is now declining.

This is partially due to the benefits being overshadowed by the rising energy and emission costs and government creating an alienating ethos that suggests industry is not valued. In addition, other countries are increasingly providing a positive impetus and actively trying to attract manufacturing companies, stacking the competition against UK industry. Fiona Ferguson recounted that one company asked the CIA: 'where is the incentive in "Renewable Heat Incentive?"' Many other countries view industry as an investment opportunity, where any initial outlay will be recouped in time. Stan Higgins suggested:

> *The emigration of businesses due to offers of incentives elsewhere has already begun.*

> If you're going to build a £350 million plant, many governments will give you £50 million to do it, because they know it's going to be there for a very long time and they will reap the benefits. Our government has never seen it like that.

The emigration of businesses due to offers of incentives elsewhere has already begun: a plastic polymer firm originally based in the UK moved to Portugal because the country was offering to pay for 20 per cent of their capital costs. As a result, the company even used its existing British workers to help construct the new Portuguese plant that would then be the cause of their redundancies. The crucial issue that the government has to remember is that many chemical firms are globally mobile and will settle wherever the best conditions are offered.

The crucial issue is that when R&D and production are based together and one leaves, the other often follows soon after. The retention of R&D is increasingly uncertain, most recently seen in the relocation of INEOS headquarters from England to Lausanne, Switzerland to save €450 million by 2014.[1] This should be unsettling to the government and proof that the current tax regime is unfavourable. Jeremy Nicholson commented: 'I'm sure there's a very good reason for this happening... but if it becomes impossible to invest here and earn a return because the future risks here are too high, this will have consequences.' The government has claimed existing R&D tax breaks are an incentive, but these only have an effect if the company pays British corporation tax, something foreign firms can reduce. Some UK subsidiaries are funded by a loan from the overseas parent, with a high interest rate. The UK subsidiary thus has high financing costs which reduce taxable income and therefore minimise UK tax, while the parent can take its profit through the interest paid. Extending R&D incentives outside of tax credits to all research activities in Britain will go a long way to restoring high-end chemical industry investment in the UK.

Foreign and multinational ownership

Many chemical firms are now foreign owned and this has created new challenges for the industry. While attracting overseas investment is a highly beneficial exercise in itself, it is also fragile and requires active nurturing from government. Like any seed, foreign investment requires agreeable conditions if it is to grow, but the current high costs and uncertainty over future ones are beginning to drive this away.

Seventy per cent of CIA members have their headquarters based overseas and most of these firms don't have anyone in the UK to make important strategic decisions, all of which have to be taken back to headquarters where people may not share the UK government's enthusiasm for high production costs. These multinational are often aware from their wider experience that Britain is more punitive towards industry than most other countries, which is a black mark when it comes to investment decisions. Fiona Ferguson stated:

> When UK site managers have to ask their bosses in Leverkusen, America or the Middle East for investment in their plants, they will be faced with awkward questions about the security of supply for gas and electricity. Their parent companies can point to the fact that the UK is at the end of the gas pipeline, has little gas storage as back-up and energy-intensive companies are extremely vulnerable to the massive spikes in energy prices we see in the UK.

The effect of this reticence can be seen in terms of net capital stock investments, which have risen, but far less sharply than they should have done—the result of multinationals channelling money into other countries instead. From 2001-09, the chemicals sector's capital stock grew at 2006 prices from £30.5 billion to £31.4 billion, a rise of just £0.9 billion.[2] The slow but steady rise in production might not

> *The decline will not happen immediately but will become apparent over time as UK chemical production is outpaced and innovation declines.*

seem bad when other manufacturing sectors have been cutting back, but compared to the total British industry growth of £530.1 billion over the same period, the growth appears disproportionately small for a sector that the UK economy relies on.[3] Stan Higgins has seen this stagnation at NEPIC:

> There is a rising cost to products, which will see less investment initially and then people will say 'oh we're not going to invest in Britain' and the current manufacturers will struggle for a while and then one by one they'll say 'we're moving production of this material to our other global locations'. We'll end up with just sales offices and warehouses here.

It is important to view this with a long-term perspective—the decline will not happen immediately but will become apparent over time as UK chemical production is outpaced and innovation declines. While everything may appear fine under the Coalition government, this is unlikely to be the case in a few years and a future government may be left to pick up the pieces.

This long-term decline is the result of the two methods of energy-saving investments chemical firms can choose from. The easier option is to make many small changes at low cost by retrofitting existing plants with carbon saving measures. This allows emissions reduction up to a point but for greater efficiency, the second choice is to build entirely new plants. The 34 per cent carbon reduction target the government desires is so high that, for most firms, only new factories will be able to deliver the necessary changes. The crucial issue is that when companies are deciding where to construct new plants, they no longer need to take the investments already made in the UK into account. Instead, the decision can be based within the global context of which country will deliver the best profits: Lucite, which was taken over by Mitsubishi Rayon in November 2008, has seen the construction of new MMA plants around the world but none in Europe. The last two built were in Singapore and China and future plants are likely to be based in the Middle East or Asia. Phil Bailey explained:

> You don't worry so much for the existing sites as they stand, you worry about the ability to attract a big future plant. The foreign owners won't say 'I'm going to close down this half-billion-pound-worth of assets', they'll say 'I'll keep running them, but for cash', and when it comes to the next MMA plant, the UK disappears off their option list... the question is, will there ever be a new plant built in Britain?

The market for MMA is growing each year by GDP plus one per cent, so the construction of other plants is not likely to lead to the closure of Lucite's British chemical works, but given the constant need to expand capacity, the UK is missing the opportunity to secure further investment and economic benefit from an already existing facility.

The climate of production appears hostile to foreign firms, minimising enthusiasm for further investment in the UK. GrowHow is one such foreign-owned company, a joint venture between the American CF Industries and Norwegian Yara International. Deborah Pritchard Jones explained:

> In the US, grants are more readily available for N_2O abatement and trading scheme benchmarks are based on average performance. It is therefore understandably very challenging to get investments sanctioned where the overwhelming majority of the risk is shouldered by the business itself and the benchmarks are, comparatively, very stringent.

It must be remembered that even if conditions for chemical production deteriorate worldwide, companies' foreign-owned assets are the most likely to be shut down. In the past, many large multinationals have shown an unwillingness to cut back on their workforce in their home country when cuts, not necessarily better ones, can be made elsewhere. The increased cost of production in Britain will expose the UK to this weakness and could mean it becomes an easy decision for firms cutting back to close their UK plants. The government should realise it cannot assume that a foreign-owned company operating in the UK will be financially supported by its parent firm *ad infinitum* when better opportunities are available elsewhere. They have no obligations or commitments to continue UK production, especially when they own similar plants in countries that are more conducive to business success.

The 'brain drain'

The problem of retaining foreign firms in the UK is compounded by the fact that on top of investments, the most able employees are also being channelled into plants in other countries, many of which are direct competitors.

The CIA organises the 'Future Forum', which is designed to acquaint the most able new employees of chemical firms with the global industry and its concerns. While many of those attending the Forum are British, a surprising number then go on to take up work abroad with multinational companies.

This high level of emigration by potential employees is to the detriment of Britain. The Government must recognise this and understand why it is happening.

Lack of awareness

The vast majority of the British public would struggle to name a single UK-based chemical company and as Fiona Ferguson put it: 'people don't know we're here. If you ask them to name a chemical company they will say ICI, but ICI began to fragment in 1992 and finally lost its identity two years ago.' Despite its contribution to the economy and society at large, the chemical industry operates without visible external media coverage or advertising. One way or another, this has to change; ignorance has led to apathy towards its continuation and there is a lack of understanding as to why the sector should not be regulated out of existence. This must involve a two-pronged approach to win over not just the public, but the civil service and politicians as well.

While the industry has been operating below the radar of public opinion, in these far tougher times there is an acute need for chemical firms to reach out and proclaim their worth. Awareness would bring support, which the industry desperately needs in dealing with the government and the EU. Stan Higgins argued:

> I think a lack of understanding in the leadership through parliament of what the industry provides and can do within society is a huge problem. The ignorance of what it provides for the country's economy and social life is incredible. It's not understood and therefore not wanted and not loved.

The lack of public awareness partly results from the chemical industry's structure. Chemical firms primarily sell to other companies within the industry, with big ones like INEOS selling their products to other smaller companies producing a variety of non-consumer goods. There is no need to appeal to the public in this, so advertising is kept to a minimum. For the majority of chemical companies, dealing with the public has so far not seemed worth the hassle, as it makes no difference to their profit. This has left a gulf filled by a media focus on the negative aspects of the industry. Fiona Ferguson said:

> The press loves a story about how dangerous chemicals are. It is very difficult to persuade them that, whilst chemical A is toxic to rats at high doses, the levels humans are exposed to are way below the risk level. This perception of the industry makes it difficult to promote the good news such as the huge impact new methods of manufacturing insulation or lighter plastics has on reducing societies' greenhouse gases.

For example, an article in the *Daily Mail* was entitled: 'The toxic timebomb: Researchers say gender-bending chemicals are rife but are they just the tip of the iceberg?'[4] Such reports are commonplace but normally inaccurate and take research out of context. The stories play off the popular myths surrounding the sector that paint a picture of safety, energy usage and pollution incompatible with a modern society reducing GHG emissions.

The responsibility for countering such myths has so far fallen to the chemical industry and their related organisations. NEPIC has been engaging in this throughout its existence but given its local community lives in the shade of chemical plants, this is far less of a challenge than informing those living without exposure to the industry such as in London and the South East. Stan Higgins said:

> It would take a huge educational effort for people to understand that their whole lives are dominated by this sector. We've battled with it for years here at NEPIC, but there's no funding for industry education. It does what it can, but this is very limited.

NEPIC and local involvement

The North East of England Process Industry Cluster is delivering a new approach to improving stakeholder relations within the North east. It has organised tours for children around local chemical plants and to great success: when asked to draw a chemical plant before the tour, the children draw smokestacks and dirty buildings but afterwards, this disappears.

In addition, NEPIC's 'Children challenging industry' program has been very successful in promoting the take-up of science courses at school, with 65 per cent of participants going on to do so. This is beneficial in the long run: a survey has found 70 per cent of engineers and scientists said they were first attracted to their future vocation while at primary school.

Given the looming problem of a skills shortage, there is a growing need for this form of activity.

Companies have shied away from telling the government how vulnerable they are to rising costs due to fears that investors, parent companies or customers might pick up on this and divert their funds elsewhere, creating even larger problems for the firm. As a result of this, the government has understandably assumed that the industry has been successfully adapting to the influx of regulations and the few speaking out are bluffing over the seriousness of the situation. Jeremy Nicholson argued:

The government reaction is always 'well until you start closing your factory doors we don't believe you', which is a bit like a doctor advising you to not worry about your heath because you're not dead yet. Up until the point you are dead that's a fair comment—but not a terribly helpful one.

The industry's unwillingness to highlight its weaknesses has created a real dilemma for many companies, barring GrowHow who have publicly voiced their concerns. Deborah Pritchard Jones said this was because: 'the situation had become so dire that GrowHow might as well let people know what its costs and structure are, it's too late not to be open'. Other chemical firms may soon follow GrowHow's example and should do so soon—the time is approaching when they will have nothing to lose. A concerted and unified effort to draw attention to this fact is the only option left.

> *The situation had become so dire that GrowHow might as well let people know what its costs and structure are, it's too late not to be open.*

Conclusion and Policy Recommendations

The statistics show how far Britain's economy relies on the chemical sector. To narrow the current record high £97.2 billion trade in goods deficit, the chemical industry must grow, especially as the financial service sector has declined in its contribution due to the recession.[1] This means that a stagnation of chemical production is as unviable an option as a decline. Taking a snapshot of the present time, the UK chemical industry appears to be in a strong position. It is still able to channel investment and can compete strongly with rival countries. Phil Bailey said:

> Fundamentally, our cost base at the moment is not that much different to manufacturing MMA in China or Singapore. If we don't do anything and we put several million on our cost base and they don't though, then it starts to fall down a slippery slope... You start to line these costs up and each on its own isn't enough to shut the site, but the cumulative impact says this isn't a really a good place to do business.

Lucite and many other UK chemical firms are at a critical juncture and require further investment to retain their competitive advantage. If investment is not given, the decline of the industry will set in.

The chemical industry is facing a threat akin to a time bomb. The government's current climate change policies may be the easiest and quickest ways to shrink the UK's carbon footprint, but they will also be the hardest to recover from, if recovery is possible at all. Once the chemicals industry has been priced out of the UK market, there will be little chance of getting it to return. This is not overemphasis or scare-mongering, but the most likely outcome of pricing Britain out of the energy-intensive manufacturing market. Jeremy Nicholson summarised:

> If you're an electro-intensive industry and you've got no means of avoiding these charges and electricity costs are anywhere between 25

per cent to 75 per cent of your production costs, it is impossible to see how such an industry could remain competitive internationally.

In addition, the present uncertainty as to the future of the taxation regime has stifled investment as this ambiguity is fed into investment risk models, and this is equally damaging in the long-term. While Britain is still gaining more chemical investment than it is losing, this trend will reverse if production costs rise. The government must realise that its self-professed goal of creating 'an environment in which businesses can thrive' will not be the outcome of pursuing current policies.[2]

Put simply, there is no need for this. The dual aims of the *Growth Review*, nurturing the LCE and boosting economic growth, can both be achieved through the chemicals sector and its downstream industries. What is now needed is for all government departments (most of all DECC) to recognise that while each has its own goals, the chemicals sector can help to achieve them all.

The status quo green policies based on levies and continually pushing up energy prices are now out-dated. Outlined below are some recommended actions for the government to consider if it really wants green growth:

1. A stable regulatory and taxation environment

Before anything else, it is important to state that the solution is not to abandon the entire system that has been built up so far. There have been clear benefits to long-term policies with general standards improved and emissions lowered throughout the chemical industry. Safety in production and during transport must also remain paramount concerns. Regulation of such a potentially hazardous industry is essential and cannot be abandoned. The crucial point, though, is that regulations should not be vastly modified once implemented.

Companies have spent millions researching how they will adapt under layer upon layer of regulation as they stand and have spent much more money implementing the changes. To alter or scrap the policies entirely would create a feeling that it was all for nothing and would be as damaging to the sector's morale as further levies. In addition, it would penalise the best performers and fastest adopters of regulations, something to be avoided as it would erode confidence and discourage rapid implementation of future policies.

The start of the EU ETS Phase III in 2013 will end the status quo over energy costs. In light of this, the government should focus on simplifying the current complex network of domestic policies. Companies must be able to see clearly what they are liable for, what charges they are exempt from, and what costs are in the pipeline– all allowing them to plan and budget accordingly. Most of all, the industry must be given the time to adjust to new costs and targets.

2. Competitive energy costs

If Vince Cable really wants 'British business to be a powerhouse for economic growth and among the most competitive in the world', he must prevent punitive green policies going too far.[3] The cost of energy is the central issue that will make or break the chemical industry. It has been shown from past experience that the industry can cope with low but still significant levels of energy taxation or levies which promote efficiency but do not jeopardise their competitive edge. This is the optimum scenario for the sector.

However, raising the cost of energy too high is ultimately going to undermine the whole sector. It will be impossible to invest in emission reducing innovations if sliding profits do not provide enough funds to allow this. If this were to happen, the loss of demand for carbon-saving measures in the UK would actually draw the remaining low-carbon businesses overseas. A counter-intuitive ending to a rushed policy.

Of course, if the government is going to stick to its guns over funding renewable sources of energy and other low-carbon initiatives it will require huge investment and revenue for this purpose. As in other countries, the solution would be general energy taxation, shifting the burden to a wider area and sharing the cost throughout the whole energy market. This would allow the government to honour its green commitments and sustain green levy income (albeit still at a high economic cost) while mitigating the damage to manufacturing sectors including chemicals. This approach also makes sense: overly burdening energy-intensive sectors is economically unwise and a general levy reflects the reality that 'we are all in it together', a phrase encapsulating the zeitgeist of many Coalition policies.

3. Push for equality of implementation across the EU and reasonable targets

The EU Industrial Emissions Directive, the EU ETS and other European-wide regulations/levies will only work if they are fairly implemented across all member states. This is not yet the case, and the British government should exert pressure to ensure that this happens. Non-compliance gives an unfair advantage to countries who are currently able to profit from their own wrongdoing.

Many member states are not yet acting properly on their commitment to reduce emissions by 20 per cent by 2020. In light of this, it is misguided of Chris Huhne and others to push further and demand the target is raised to 30 per cent. Few of the largest polluting countries will agree to this and even if it is adopted, the UK's 34 per cent target is still unilaterally higher. British industries will pay the hefty price.

Europe cannot be divorced from its global context: overly raising costs could create a scenario where the EU as a whole loses chemical investments and companies on an epic scale. This benefits no one, especially since the EU has implemented many positive safety and environmental regulations unlikely to be found anywhere else. Pushing the sector out of the EU could set the responsible nature of companies back decades.

Like many regulations, REACH is bound to have teething troubles as guidance is interpreted and companies find their own circumstances in real life are unaccounted for. This means there is a crucial need to continue to be pragmatic in their implementation and keep an open dialogue with the industry to find mutually satisfactory solutions. Similarly, the success of the British chemicals sector is often due to its unique products and methods, something not always accounted for by EU blanket rules. While these are normally altered on a painstakingly slow timetable, the UK government should fight the industry's corner when possible. Such a move would encourage innovation and cement Britain's reputation as a world leader for chemical R&D.

4. No unilateral levies

In theory, the whole world could agree to raise the cost of energy equally and universally. However desirable, this remains a dream and the reality of the situation cannot be ignored. Britain must remain economically viable.

> *Raising British energy costs above those of other countries is economic suicide.*

Raising British energy costs above those of other countries is economic suicide. The carbon price floor is at the centre of this, not least because the minimum tariff appears to be £30/tCO$_2$, the price at which many in the chemical industry see the 'point of no return', where business emigration will begin *en-masse*.

The desire to 'lead on climate change' and to be 'ahead of the pack' in an international context is best served by not ruining the UK's industries. Pricing them into exile will be tantamount to shooting Britain in the foot on an epic scale.

The more responsible approach would be to recognise that Britain can best serve the interests of the global fight against climate change by producing the products that the rest of the world can use to reduce their own emissions more effectively. Indeed, it is environmentally sensible to maintain a competitive and dynamic market that would attract energy-intensive LCE companies to settle in the UK.

5. Aim to foster long-term low-carbon growth

It is absolutely critical that the chemicals sector be seen as part of the LCE and the 'greenest government ever' will presumably be looking to take advantage of the reduction in emissions that it can deliver. However, this needs to be seen in terms of maximising the *volume* of the reductions, not the *speed* at which they are to happen. Having seen how the products of the chemicals sector are vital to reducing GHGs, the industry must be allowed to thrive.

Future environmental policies need to take into consideration more than just the emissions output of sectors. Taxing the quantity of energy used or the emissions released during production is not an accurate reflection of actual poll- ution. Basic chemicals like chlorine might appear surplus to require- ments when taken out of context,

> *Without the chemical industry, the low-carbon economy will perish in its infancy.*

but there needs to be a realisation that without British production of basic chemicals, there would also be no British wind turbines or British electric cars which rely on them. Similarly, the industry is too interdependent to allow only certain products such as insulation materials to escape high costs: it is a case of all or nothing. Without the chemical industry, the low-carbon economy will perish in its infancy.

Further emission reductions will rely on technologies that require high investment and long-term development; PYReco's tyre pyrolysis took 12 years to develop. Some of these bigger changes will also need entirely new plants when retrofitting is not possible. This in itself will force many firms to reassess whether to continue UK production, when a harsh green tax regime with associated add-on charges will not be looked on kindly.

6. Foster a positive atmosphere for industry

The chemicals sector is still viewed through a lens of stereotypes and out-dated assumptions. The mentality behind the energy and emissions tax regime assumes that the industry is quite content with polluting; this is simply wrong. In 1990, the chemical industry had an output of 48.2 Mt CO_2e for all GHGs. In 2008 this figure was 12.6 Mt CO_2e, a reduction of just under 74 per cent.[4] Clearly, the industry has been doing its part (even discounting the low-carbon value of its products) and at a phenomenal rate. It has already gone further than the 20 per cent required reduction, or even the proposed 30 per cent! While punitive taxes might have kick-started this reduction and allowed the easiest changes to be made, future progress will rely on a cooperative, rather than confrontational, attitude from government.

The industry must be seen in a new perspective—not as an undesirable burden but as an investment opportunity and valued by the country accordingly. The UK is almost unique for not having this mentality—so many other countries are proud of their manufacturing sectors and welcome the chance to develop them further.

Pragmatically and ideologically; economically and environmentally, there is every reason to nurture the chemicals sector.

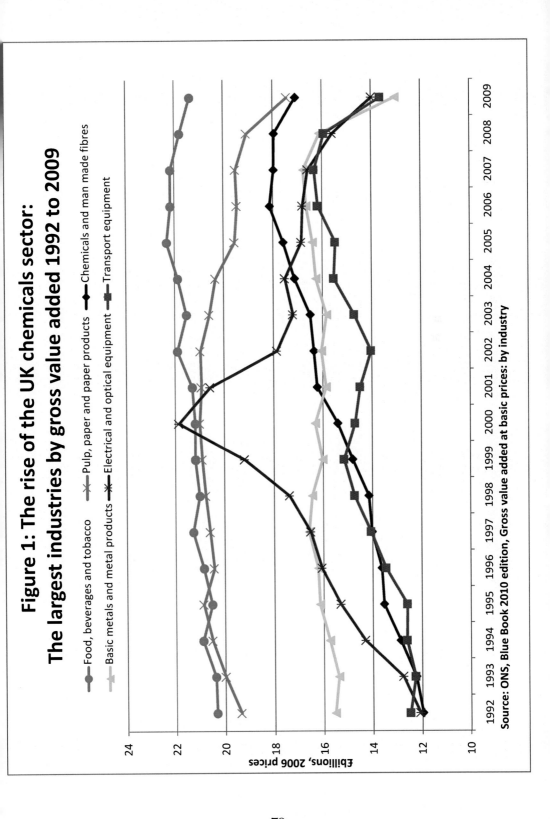

Figure 1: The rise of the UK chemicals sector:
The largest industries by gross value added 1992 to 2009

Food, beverages and tobacco — Pulp, paper and paper products — Chemicals and man made fibres

Basic metals and metal products — Electrical and optical equipment — Transport equipment

£billions, 2006 prices

24 22 20 18 16 14 12 10

1992 1993 1994 1995 1996 1997 1998 1999 2000 2001 2002 2003 2004 2005 2006 2007 2008 2009

Source: ONS, Blue Book 2010 edition, Gross value added at basic prices: by industry

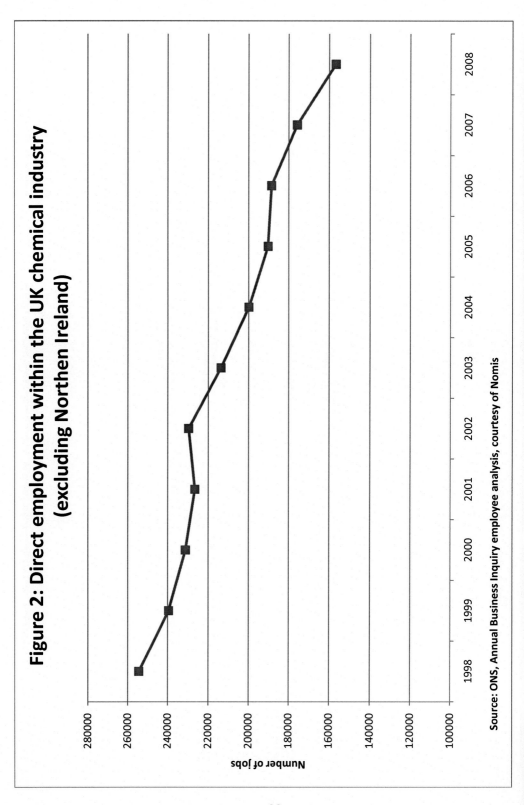

Figure 2: Direct employment within the UK chemical industry (excluding Northen Ireland)

Number of jobs

Source: ONS, Annual Business Inquiry employee analysis, courtesy of Nomis

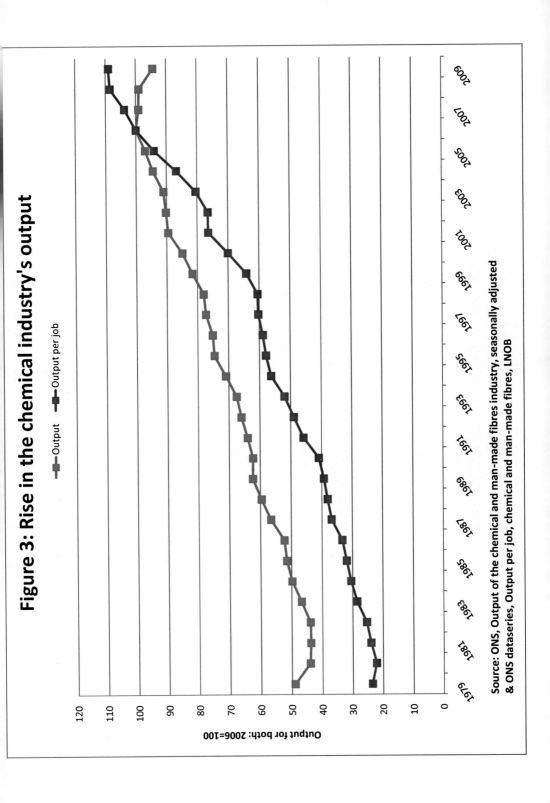

Figure 3: Rise in the chemical industry's output

Output   Output per job

Output for both: 2006=100

1979 1981 1983 1985 1987 1989 1991 1993 1995 1997 1999 2001 2003 2005 2007 2009

Source: ONS, Output of the chemical and man-made fibres industry, seasonally adjusted
& ONS dataseries, Output per job, chemical and man-made fibres, LNOB

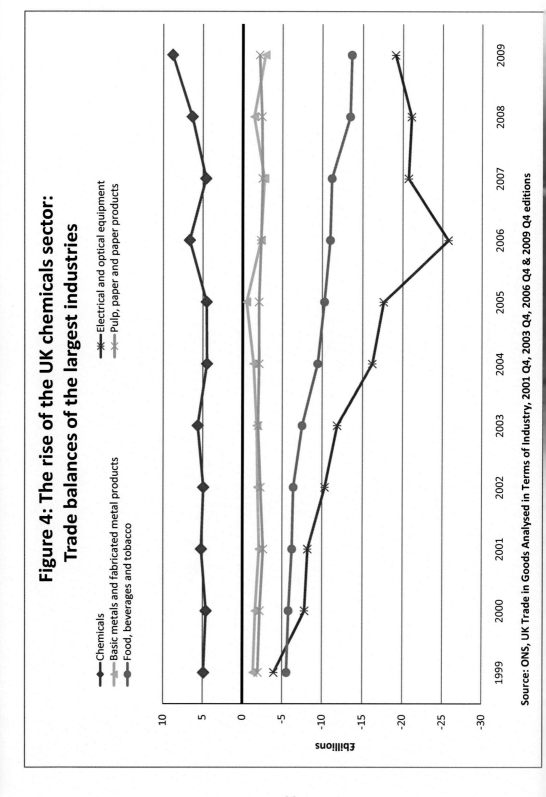

Figure 4: The rise of the UK chemicals sector:
Trade balances of the largest industries

Legend:
- Chemicals
- Basic metals and fabricated metal products
- Food, beverages and tobacco
- Electrical and optical equipment
- Pulp, paper and paper products

£billions

Source: ONS, UK Trade in Goods Analysed in Terms of Industry, 2001 Q4, 2003 Q4, 2006 Q4 & 2009 Q4 editions

Figure 5: The cumulative impact of climate change policies on an energy-intensive user's costs

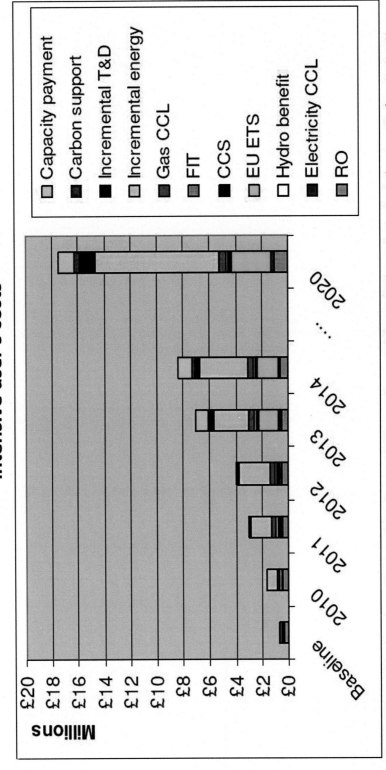

Source: Waters Wye Associates, The Cumulative Impact of Climate Change Policies on UK Energy Intensive Industries - Update Against New Government Policy, March 2011, p. 3

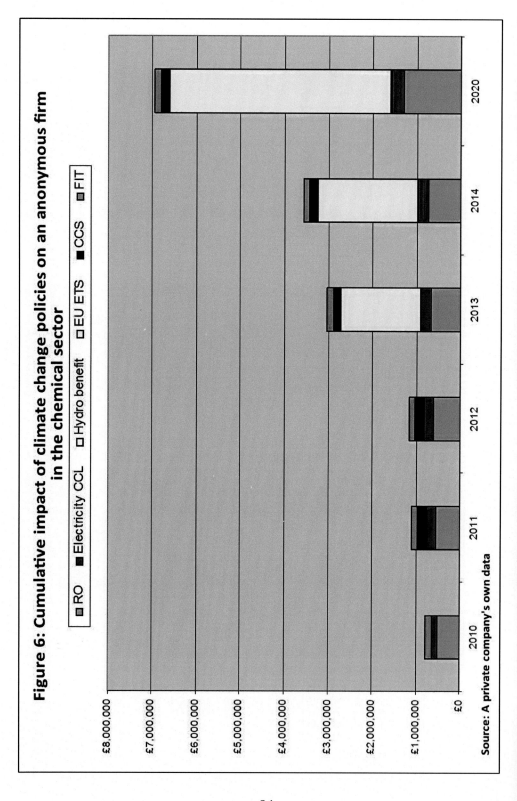

Figure 6: Cumulative impact of climate change policies on an anonymous firm in the chemical sector

Source: A private company's own data

84

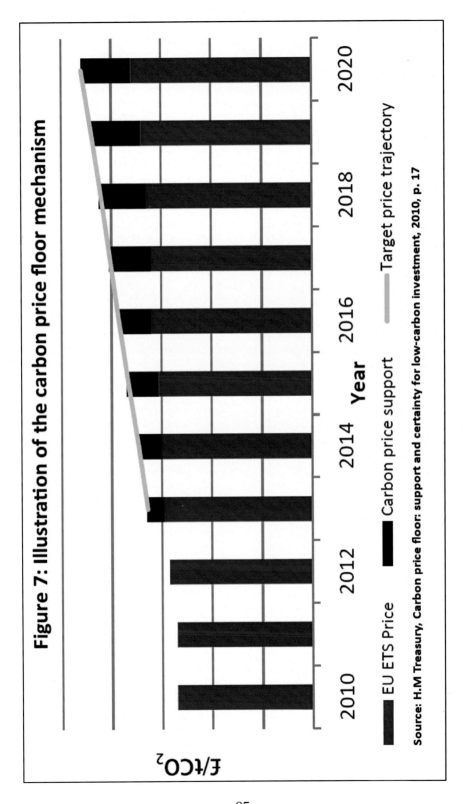

Figure 7: Illustration of the carbon price floor mechanism

EU ETS Price ■ Carbon price support ■ Target price trajectory

Year

£/tCO$_2$

2010   2012   2014   2016   2018   2020

Source: H.M Treasury, Carbon price floor: support and certainty for low-carbon investment, 2010, p. 17

Notes

Introduction

1 http://www.decc.gov.uk/en/content/cms/
   what_we_do/lc_uk/carbon_budgets/carbon_budgets.aspx

2 http://www.decc.gov.uk/en/content/cms/
   what_we_do/uk_supply/energy_mix/renewable/res/res.aspx

3 DECC, *UK Renewable Energy Strategy 2009: overall impact assessment*, July
   2009, pp. 2-5.

4 Lea, R. & Nicholson, N., *British Energy Policy and the Threat to
   Manufacturing Industry*, London: Civitas, July 2010, p. 2.

5 Different technologies are awarded different quantities of ROC e.g.
   offshore wind power receives 2 ROCs per MWh.

6 OFGEM, *The Renewables Obligation Buy-Out Price and Mutualisation
   Ceiling 2010-11: information note*, February 2010, p. 1.

7 Waters Wye Associates, *The Cumulative Impact of Climate Change Policies
   on UK Energy Intensive Industries: a summary report*, July 2010, p. 5.

8 Office for National Statistics, *Index of Production*, data for manufacturing,
   CKYY + QTPR.

9 Oxford Economics, *The Economic Benefits of Chemistry Research to the UK*,
   September 2010, p. 3.

10 Chemical Industry Association, *Chemical and Pharmaceutical Businesses in
   the UK: our campaigns*, September 2010, p. 4.

11 *The Economic Benefits of Chemistry Research to the UK*, p. 3.

12 http://www.ineoschlor.com/efw/energyfromwaste.shtml

13 DECC, *Phase II National Allocation Plan (2008-12)*, Appendix E, Tables III
   & IV, 2008-12 average.

14 BIS, *Growth Review: the path to strong, sustainable and balanced growth*,
   November 2010; and BIS, *Growth Review Framework for Advanced
   Manufacturing*, December 2010.

15 *Growth Review*, p. 22.

16 *Growth Review*, p. 10.

17 *Growth Review*, p. 16.

18 *Growth Review*, p. 5.

19 *Growth Review Framework*, p. 6.

1: The Past: The Consequences of Existing Policies

1 Huhne, C., Speech at the ippr conference on 1 December 2010, Q&A session;
   http://www.ippr.org/feeds/files/2010_12_01_NEE_launch_Chris_Huhne.mp3

2 Huhne, C., Speech.

3 http://www.decc.gov.uk/en/content/cms/what_we_do/lc_uk/crc/crc.aspx

4 *Telegraph*, 'Fury over £1bn green stealth tax in spending review', 20 October 2010.

5 http://ec.europa.eu/enterprise/sectors/chemicals/reach/index_en.htm

6 DECC, *The Carbon Plan*, March 2011, p. 33, Box 4.1.

7 Chemical Industries Association, *The Chemical Industry: delivering a low-carbon future 24 hours a day*, 2010, p. 9.

8 *Business Green*, 'DECC opens door for CCS gas plants', 8 November 2010.

2: The Present: Britain is Pricing Itself Out of the Market

1 CQuestCapital, *CQC's view of supply and demand in the CDM offset market*, May 2010, p. 5.

2 http://www.cia.org.uk/policy-issue-details.php?id=4

3 http://nds.coi.gov.uk/content/Detail.aspx?ReleaseID=417079&NewsAreaID=2

4 Huhne, C., Speech at the ippr conference on 1 December 2010.

5 *Power-Gen Worldwide*, 'How will the EU ETS shape the European power generation mix?', Vol. 18, No. 7, August 2010.

6 HM Treasury, *Carbon Price Floor: support and certainty for low-carbon investment*, December 2010.

7 HM Treasury, *Carbon Price Floor, Summary: intervention and options*, 16 December 2010, p. 3.

8 *Carbon Price Floor, Summary*, p. 4.

9 HM Revenue & Customs, *Carbon Price Floor: tax information and impact note*, 23 March 2011, p. 5.

10 DECC, *Estimated Impacts of Energy and Climate Change Policies on Energy Prices and Bills*, July 2010, p. 20.

3: The Future: How the Low-carbon Economy is being Jeopardised

1 Cameron, D., Speech at the Department of Energy and Climate Change, 14 May 2010.

2 ONS, *The Blue Book: 2010 Edition*, p. 279, chart 13.9.

3 Waters Wye Associates, *The Cumulative Impact of Climate Change Policies on UK Energy Intensive Industries: a summary report*, July 2010, p. 47

4 http://www.letsrecycle.com/news/latest-news/waste-management/health-concerns-in-debate-over-ps300m-incinerator

5 Huhne, C., Speech at the ippr conference on 1 December 2010.

6 Chemical Industries Association, *The Chemical Industry: delivering a low-carbon future 24 hours a day*, 2010, p. 15.

7 *The Cumulative Impact*, p. 47

8 *Delivering a low-carbon future*, p.5

9 BIS, *Growth Review: the path to strong, sustainable and balanced growth*, November 2010, p. 22.

10 *Delivering a low-carbon future*, p. 5

11 http://www.wrap.org.uk/wrap_corporate/about_wrap/index.html

12 http://www.decc.gov.uk/en/content/cms/news/eu_cc_article/
eu_cc_article.aspx

4: The Wider Picture: The Downstream Effect

1 Royal Society of Chemistry, *The Economic Benefits of Chemistry: summary report*, September 2010, p. 2.

2 *The Economic Benefits of Chemistry*, p. 2.

3 Training and Employment Research Unit & Public and Corporate Economic Consultants, *Teesside Petrochemical Complex Socio-Economic Impact Study: executive summary*, 2003, p. 3.

4 ONS, *UK Business: Activity, Size and Location*, 2010 edn, Table B2.1.

5 Huhne, C., Speech at the ippr conference on 1 December 2010.

6 *The Times*, 'Wilton threat is "hammer blow for North East"', 1 August 2009.

5: A Level Playing Field?

1 http://www.ineos.com/new_item.php?id_press=268

2 ONS, *Capital Stocks, Capital Consumption and Non-Financial Balance Sheets*, 2010, Table 1.2.2.

3 *Capital Stocks*, Table 1.2.2.

4 http://www.dailymail.co.uk/health/article-1262143/The-toxic-timebomb-Researchers-say-gender-bending-chemicals-rife-just-tip-iceberg.html

Conclusion and Policy Recommendations

1 ONS, *Statistical Bulletin: UK Trade*, December 2010, February 2011, p. 2.

2 BIS, *Growth Review: the path to strong, sustainable and balanced growth*, November 2010, p. 14.

3 http://nds.coi.gov.uk/content/Detail.aspx?ReleaseID=417079&NewsAreaID=2

4 ONS, *Environmental Accounts: emissions; greenhouse gases, 93 industries*, total emissions, sectors 20-28.